Russian Houses

Russian Houses

Elizabeth Gaynor | Kari Haavisto
with essays by Darra Goldstein

EVERGREEN

The authors wish to give special thanks to the following: Finnair, Ksenia Berezovskaya, Jessica Ertman, Barbara Finamore, Roy Finamore, Deborah Geltman, Lina Gorelik, Natasha Kaufman, Margaret Kennedy, Vasily Popov, Sol Shulman, Marie Stock, J. C. Suarès, Galena Udod, Nina Ulfand and May Britt Virolainen.

Page 2: the central stairway and grand chandelier in the Yusupov palace; *Page 5:* an *izba* currently inhabited in the village of Polenova; *Page 6:* a neoclassical detail seen between the seventeenth-century towers of the Znamensky Cathedral in Moscow; *Page 8:* the country baroque trim of a timber house at Kizhi, *Page 11:* the interior of a nineteenth-century log house at Kizhi; *Page 12:* a windmill built in 1928 by Nikolai Bikanin from the village of Volkostrov; *Page 56:* portals of a fifteenth-century church in Moscow; *Page 59:* two griffins standing guard at the end of the Bankovsky Bridge over the Griboyedov Canal in Leningrad; *Page 60:* statues in the Summer Garden of Peter the Great; *Page 126:* in the living room of early-twentieth-century actress Maria Yermolova; *Page 129:* late-nineteenth-century Slavic Revival house, now the French Embassy in Moscow; *Page 130:* a suite of nineteenth-century Karelian birch furniture in the Empire style; *Page 216:* a Moscow apartment building built in 1949–53 in the style popularly called Stalin Gothic; *Page 219:* a Muscovite immersed in his newspaper on the balcony of his apartment; *Page 220:* a neighborhood of contemporary *izbas* in Suzdal.

This book was printed on 100% chlorine-free bleached paper in accordance with the TCF standard.

EVERGREEN is a label of Benedikt Taschen Verlag GmbH

Printed in Italy
ISBN 3–8228–9049–9
GB

CONTENTS

CHAPTER 1

PROVINCIAL LIFE

PROVINCIAL LIFE

ACROSS THE RUSSIAN NORTH stretch dense forests, home to bears and wolves. These dark, seemingly impenetrable woods frightened the early settlers, who imagined evil spirits lurking among the trees. Overcoming their fears, the Russians set out to tame the wilderness and turn it to their advantage. The cottages they built at the edge of the trees provided shelter from the buffeting arctic winds, and once hewn into logs, the ominous trees became a source of warmth and light.

Even on the threshold of the twenty-first century, the wooden cottage, or *izba,* remains deeply rooted in the Russian psyche as a symbol of simplicity and comfort that also represents an aesthetic, even spiritual, perception of the world. These cottages served to diminish and humanize the vast scale of the Russian landscape, offering a place of comfort in an alien universe, a refuge from the cold, and an assertion of themselves.

The Russian cottage is designed to highlight the best properties of the wood used in building it. A genuine *izba* accentuates the wood's color, grain, and texture and in so doing reflects an organic outgrowth of nature. Pine, fir, and spruce were the woods of choice, not only for their accessibility and relative softness, but for their beauty. Pine radiates a yellow light beside fir's silvery hue, especially striking in the pale sun of winter. The rough-hewn logs

acquired a rich patina as they aged, causing the cottage to glow and exude warmth, features much appreciated in such a bleak climate. Through imaginative juxtapositions, the Russians enhanced the innate properties of the different woods, particularly in the interiors of their cottages. Thus, they prized aspen for its light color and uniform texture as a counterpoint to the more pronounced grains of the conifers. Only in the eighteenth century did the Russians begin to follow European fashion by disguising the true nature of wood under stucco and elaborate trompe l'oeil patterns. But the *izba* hearkens back to an earlier, more purely Russian aesthetic and functions as a kind of icon for a whole range of deeply felt values.

The Russians worked the wood in the most natural ways, avoiding what they considered superfluous technology. Even into the twentieth century they preferred to build their cottages with an axe rather than a saw. Experience showed that logs hewn with an axe absorbed less moisture than the smoother faces of saw-milled planks, making the wood less susceptible to warp and rot. Still, the ease of handling planks instead of logs was too tempting for some builders to resist, and after the sawmill was introduced around 1676, a number of framed houses were constructed. Carpenters also availed themselves of both old and new technologies by casing logs

with milled boards. The Russian peasant continued to prefer log construction for aesthetic reasons, however, finding that the uneven play of light across the logs lent character and depth to the dwelling. Boards were simply too uniform, and too new, to offer the same interest.

The individuality of a cottage depended on the size and type of log used rather than on a given architectural design, since the construction of the *izba* was virtually the same throughout the Russian north. The Russians fitted the logs together by layering or interlocking them, shunning iron nails in favor of wooden dowels or spikes. To keep out the cold they stuffed the chinks between logs with moss and sometimes covered the decorative wooden roof shingles with sod or birch bark for further insulation. Thus, even the earliest dwellings were fairly airtight.

For a poorer family such excellent construction proved to be a problem, since there was no place for the smoke from the large Russian stove to escape. Used for heating and cooking, the stove featured prominently in every cottage, no matter how simple. Cottages without ventilation were called "black" from the soot that covered the ceilings and walls. Wealthier families who could afford flues for their stoves lived in "white" cottages. The roofs of these cottages were topped with ornately carved wooden stovepipes, lending the structures a fairy-tale look.

The traditional cottage afforded not only physical protection, but also a defense against the spiritual terrors of the larger world. Russians believed their households were guarded by a *domovoi*, a generally benevolent spirit that could wreak havoc or even desert the home when angered. The reassuring presence of the *domovoi* stood in marked contrast to the presence of the forest spirits, known to accost unwary foragers and hunters. To gain extra protection, families often carved wooden figures to decorate the gable ends of their roofs. These carvings represented a deep belief in the power of imagery to ward off evil. Typical designs included the *sirin*—half-maiden, half-bird, with tail feathers and breasts—and the sun, meant to shine good fortune on all.

By crafting materials from the forbidding natural world to meet their own needs, the superstitious Russians buttressed themselves against their terrors. The interiors of their cottages also contained symbolic elements. Most prominent was the *krasny ugol,* or "beautiful corner," where icons were hung and guests were seated in honor. Diagonally across from this corner stood the massive masonry stove, the only nonwooden structure in the cottage. With candles or a lamp always burning under the icons, the beautiful corner radiated a companion warmth to the stove, suffusing the entire cottage with a glow despite its lack of natural light.

In summer and fall, Russians filled their cottages with wild flowers and herbs, hung to dry for the cold season ahead. In winter they decorated the room with fresh pine boughs. In place of curtains, sprigs of cranberries and mountain ash berries were arranged in the windows, which were kept from steaming up by pieces of moisture-absorbent charcoal. The stove's heat released the fragrance of pine from the boughs, making the air redolent with the scent of winter. Even passersby could enjoy the coziness of the winter cottage, cheered by the bright reds and greens framed in the windows and backlit by the glow of the icon lamp. Unfortunately, this inviting tableau belied the constant risk of fire. Few wooden buildings remain today.

Like the exterior of the *izba*, the interior was made almost entirely of wood, including the furnishings. Benches for sitting and sleeping stretched along the entire length of the walls opposite the stove; the family elders had the privilege of sleeping on a special platform right on top of the stove. A fixed counter was usually built near the front door. Sometimes a wooden partition separated the cooking area around the stove from the rest of the cottage, but more often all activity took place in one central room. Most of the furniture was built-in for efficient use of the limited space and as household design developed in Russia and furnishings became more elaborate, movable furniture came to indicate a bourgeois home.

The furniture and utensils were usually fancifully carved and frequently painted in bright colors, as were the dwelling's ceiling beams and trim work. Woodcuts, primitive engravings, or pictures clipped from popular magazines embellished the walls along with embroidered towels displayed on holders. The embroidery designs might be mythological, geometric, or taken from nature, as the Russians often surrounded themselves with mimetic suns, trees, horses, and birds.

These natural and geometric forms were repeated in the intricate exterior carvings—of window frames, roof edgings, corner moldings, pediments, gables, lintels, jambs, porches, and gates—by peasants who understood the essence of the wood they worked and strove to enhance it. The styles ranged from classical to baroque, from abstract to anthropomorphic. Most often the carving was done in deep relief, providing a decorative touch to the long expanse of wall. Sometimes, though, the entire façade of a house was hand-cut with channeled or fluted facets, reminiscent of the faceted stone carvings of early Muscovy.

Because wood is inherently warm, not dank like stone, Russians considered it the healthier building material, and so wood construction persisted well into the twentieth century. Stone, however, has the advantage of being impervious to fire and rot. Therefore, boulders, when available, were used for foundations in place of the tarred stumps that were an early attempt at treated wood. A boulder was placed at each corner of the foundation so that the cottage was set up on piers of sorts. The result, however, enabled the wind to whip through the open space underneath. So the Russians constructed a double floor, with an insulating layer of earth packed between the "black" subfloor and the "white," or clean, floor of the cottage.

The standard cottage evolved into a simple one-room dwelling built above a lower story that served as anything from a crawl space for storage to a full story for habitation. The most common shape was the *piatistenok,* or five-walled cottage, in which a fifth interior wall was built to separate heated space from an unheated anteroom. Any number of other rooms—passageways, entry halls, lean-tos, or attics—could be appended to this basic unit. The guiding principle was to use heated and unheated space judiciously, depending on seasonal needs. This concept was carried beyond the home into public spaces, where each community had a "warm," or heatable, church for winter and a "cold" one for summer.

Climate dictated much of the *izba*'s design. To avoid going outdoors in winter, the Russians attached subsidiary buildings to the basic cottage, creating not just a large house, but an extended compound, lacking any apparent symmetry. House, hayloft, barn, and steam bath made up a random, somewhat chaotic, cluster of united buildings. Because outbuildings were attached to the basic unit depending on the owner's whim—and often with roofs of different styles—Russian villages never looked monotonous, or even orderly. Church architecture too adopted this practice of adding on, and the subsidiary buildings of many old wooden churches contribute to their fanciful air.

One ingenious aspect of the cottage was its modularity and mobility. No matter how complex the structure, a rotted board could be removed and replaced without damaging the entire structure. More important, if families decided to move (as during the upheavals of the late nineteenth century and the Revolution masses of peasants migrated to the cities), they could easily dismantle the cottage and reassemble it, particularly if it had been built in the traditional way, without nails. Wood became an increasingly expensive and scarce building material in urban areas, so even if a family chose not to reassemble the old house, its component parts could be sold for profit. The practicality of the cottage was such that Moscow once boasted a suburb called *Skorodom,* or "Quick House," which specialized in supplying materials for easily assembled wooden houses—the precursors of today's prefabs.

With all these advantages, it would seem surprising that wood should go out of style, particularly since forests are still plentiful in Russia. But the Revolution brought about a drive to modernize, and the government was eager to use more distinctively modern materials, appropriate to the image of a new and progressive society. Cast concrete, glass, and steel became the hallmarks of the new age, and the poetry of the cottage gave way to the chillier products of industry. But the Russian feeling for the *izba* endures, particularly in the countryside, where one finds brightly decorated houses and whimsically painted fences. The cottage lives on too in the traditional grave markers patterned after *izba*s. Mounted on posts, these small gabled houses figuratively provide the spirit both protection from and unity with the environment. Thus the Russian peasant lived for centuries, in a dwelling that reflected the natural world even as it kept it at bay.

15

KIZHI

IN THE NORTHWESTERN PROVINCE OF Karelia, simple ornamentation was raised to a high art. Nearly every surface is touched in some way on the ample timber structures preserved as an ensemble on the island of Kizhi there. The many buildings moved to the island from the area in the 1950s are a tribute to peasant ingenuity in this distant but important church district. At first sighting across the calm waters of Lake Onega, the restored churches, log homes, and farm buildings of Kizhi form an indelible visual imprint.

The surrounding conifer forests served not only as the prime source material for building, but also as a buffer against outsiders and their influences, allowing for the continuity of woodworking techniques through the centuries. Further, this provincial territory was long under the sovereignty of Novgorod the Great, a town famous for its carpenters, which ensured the deftness and durability of its buildings.

Through clever structural maneuvering, dwellings here managed to house extended families, workrooms, food stores, and agriculture and livestock shelters all under one roof, yielding a covered space of up to one hundred thousand cubic feet. Climate was a major factor in determining such a plan: under the one roof, work could continue without interruption throughout the severe winter months. Carved and pierced wooden trim, some as delicate as lace, was intended to enhance the play of light across the monotone façades of the bulky, unpainted homesteads, adding beauty to utility.

Interior spaces were laid out in railroad configuration under a long pitched roof or organized in a square formation. Fittings were generally simple, but freestanding furniture conveyed prosperity and was made as elaborately as the inhabitants could afford. The rooms at Kizhi illustrate the Russian propensity for decoration, interpreted in a territory where resources were scanty, by means of axe, paint, and stitchery.

The fortified enclave of timber cathedrals at Kizhi, left, includes the extraordinary twenty-two-domed Church of the Transfiguration, built in 1714, the only multi-domed church that survives from the era of Peter the Great. The Church of the Intercession was built next to it fifty years later as a winter, or heated, church. A bell tower completes the ensemble.

■

A detail of the Church of the Transfiguration shows the texture achieved through the overlapping of notched shingles on the onion domes and bochki, the decorative gables that appear to shadow the domes, opposite.

■

16

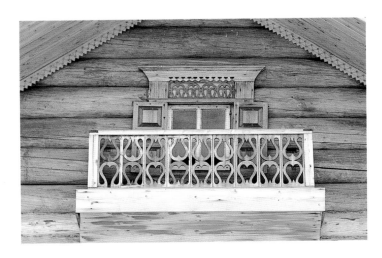

Wood was a highly expressive material to northern Russians, symbolic of their deep tie to nature and appropriate for many uses. Lengths of hand-hewn, interlocking logs set an architectural standard and unified the look of a whole village. The Serguin house, above, is a common, boxy koshel (purse) Karelian house.

■

People lived on two floors, in the more orna-mental sections of such structures, with livestock housed under the rear projection. Infinite variety in carved window frames and balustrades played against the massive scale of the exteriors and deliberately contoured them with sun and shadow. Sun swirls carved into the roof trim represented the victory of light over darkness.

■

Livestock entered the house through an arched opening in the rear section. The agricultural parts of dwellings and the outbuildings had simpler detailing.

■

The iconostasis of the Church of the Intercession is a handsome piece of northern folk art, framed by the all-timber interior, opposite. Such work was accomplished by peasants, artisans, or monks with no formal training.

■

A large samovar and the wall of painted paneled cupboards, preceding pages, *proudly announced the level of affluence of the family who lived in this house. The decoration of such pieces as the distaff from a spinning wheel leaning against one wall was a show of skill.*

The interiors, above, *reveal how bits of color could lighten dim wood rooms. Diverse patterns in embroidery, patchwork, and crochet are evidence of work accomplished on long winter days before the fire.*

■

Furnishings from the 1930s (when this house was last inhabited) that have been kept intact include a rag coverlet topped with a sheepskin throw for added warmth, family photos, and an old phonograph, *bottom right. A baby's walker and carved toys are seen, above left. In a corner of one room a draped cradle is hung by a mother's* bed, opposite, *while the space was also used for work and meals.*

■

Overleaf: *The furniture's simple lines were enhanced by painting in solid hues. A cookery corner with a preserving barrel, mixing stick, and sour-milk dishes remains as in the 1930s.*

PETER THE GREAT'S CABIN

THE WHITE SEA, KEPT PASSABLE EVEN in winter by the warm currents of the Gulf Stream, was northern Russia's main trading link with Europe for centuries and its only direct outlet to the ocean before territory on the Baltic Sea was won. Early battles of the Great Northern War (1700–1721), which pitted Russia against the kingdom of Sweden, were fought near Arkhangelsk, a strategic town by the White Sea, south of the Arctic Circle. In 1702 Peter the Great made camp here as commander in chief of the Russian navy, to oversee the fleet and the construction of an important fortress. He had a cabin built for himself on Markov Island, an island adjacent to the Novodvinskaya fortress and resided there for about two and a half months. In 1936 the house was moved to the grounds of the Kolomenskoe restoration on the outskirts of Moscow, where it was refurbished.

The cabin is an example of early-eighteenth-century architecture and also a precursor to the timber house, or *izba*, of similar proportions built for the czar when St. Petersburg was founded in 1703. The interior spaces are set up as they were used in the period, but none of the original furnishings remain. The fittings in the house today range in vintage from Peter the Great's time to the late eighteenth century.

26

The emperor's study contains a desk of the period and the sorts of accoutrements befitting his needs as commander of the navy. A wooden ship's model hangs from the ceiling on one side of the room.

■

Overleaf: Peter the Great and his guests dined in the svetlitsa, or "front room," the fanciest room of the house. The juxtaposition of decorative objects and fine textiles—some imported from Europe—against the untreated timber walls and plain window frames, gives an exceptional character to the abode. Icons shine from a corner in each room.

■

*T*he exterior of the house, top left, *built by local carpenters, shows a basic double gable construction. Log houses were built to be easily moved; timbers were numbered and reassembled according to plan. This one was relo-*cated once near Arkhangelsk before its move to the Moscow area.

■

The bed, bottom left, is from the early eighteenth century; its canopy was fashioned from an old cupboard. The coverlet is a 1913 addition.

Painted, carved cupboards sit atop the built-in benches against two walls of the dining room, above right and opposite. Some of the glass and pewter flasks are from the period.

■

NOVGOROD TIMBER HOUSES

THE TIMBER ARCHITECTURE RESTORAtion outside Novgorod comprises several houses, or *izbas*, and churches, all brought to the site from provincial surroundings. The tent-roofed churches have wooden onion domes and wraparound porches. The covered porches filled a practical need in inclement weather and also served as platforms for public speaking and meetings. Churches often served as civic arenas in country settings.

The houses, although typically not as large as those in Karelia, did provide space for food stores, hay lofts, a sled, and a few animals, as well as for the family, under one roof. Two essentials always found a place in such *izbas*: a large stove that was stoked daily and at least one icon. Sleeping was often consigned to benches, the space atop the stove, and straw mattresses on the floor nearby, so that even an actual bed was a sign of distinction. Children slept in the loft.

The main room of the house served several functions, including sleeping, dining, and working. The area by the stove was sometimes referred to as the "woman's corner," being the main area of food preparation and a warm place for doing handwork by the firelight on dim days.

32

Visitors can romp on wooden swings in Novgorod's museum village, right. Two sixteenth-century churches are seen beyond an izba, or "log house," from the village of Ryshevo, built in the nineteenth century, opposite top. Their elaborate promenade galleries and porches enlarged the structures and turned them into social gathering places. A detail of the covered stairs leading to one church, opposite bottom.

The extent of fancy carving on the izba can be seen, opposite and overleaf. A horse on the main gable was thought to bring peace to a house. Shutters, used against winter winds and the white light of summer nights, eventually evolved into pure ornament. Carved window frames were a poor man's version of expensive masonry effects; the scrollwork here is dubbed "Russian baroque."

*O*n the second story of the izba, *the main room served all functions, opposite. The* krasny ugol, *or "beautiful corner," was the name given the place in the house where the icon hung. A variety of cooking and serving vessels are placed on the table-*top for display. An accordion sits on one bench.

■

Built-in benches on the far side of the table could sleep a number of family members and there was also at least one bed under a loft platform used for storage, above. Linens greatly enhanced and softened the log interior and festive occasions called for hanging quantities of embroidered work. Clothing hangs on pegs near the bed. A carved chest contained more linens, which were rotated seasonally.

■

NOVGOROD TIMBER HOUSES

*T*he loom was an important fixture, but unlike a spinning wheel (carved as a show of skill), its appearance was largely utilitarian, above left. Embroidery patterns were innumerable, and virtually no household textile went untouched. Red and white were traditional colors, while white-on-white work was reserved for special pieces. Belts, a shirt collar, and hand towels hang on display, above right.

∎

A small side room was used for food preparation. A table there, opposite, holds storage vessels for liquids and preserves.

STATIONMASTER'S HOUSE

THIS COUNTRY PINK ENCLAVE WAS ES-tablished as a museum house based upon a story from literature. Alexander Pushkin wrote "The Stationmaster" in 1830, about the kidnapping of a stationmaster's daughter from her family home, depicting this changing station in Vyra, which he had visited many times. The name of the fictitious stationmaster, Samson Vyrin, is thought to be a variation on the village's name.

The Vyra post station, built in 1800, was the third station south from St. Petersburg. By mid-century it consisted of two masonry buildings, two stables, sheds, a blacksmith's shop, a barn, and a cobbled courtyard, all enclosed by a wall with a wooden entry gate. Here travelers changed their troika horses, warmed themselves by the fire, or refreshed themselves at the inn next door.

The interior is characteristic of a nineteenth-century post station where the warmth of provincial family life was sparked by the comings and goings of worldly visitors en route to or from the capital. Many of the furnishings of the restored station have been donated by villagers since the museum opened in 1972.

The bed has been draped as Pushkin described it, "with bright colored curtain." Chests, suitcases, "pots of balsam" on the windowsills, and framed popular prints on the walls were chosen following the writer's prose. The setting is fit for the station-master in his "long green frock coat adorned with three medals hanging from faded ribbons" to enter the house and call for his daughter, Dunya, to ready the samovar for tea.

A n entry with a bit of neoclassical detailing leads to the changing station from the old Petersburg road, below.

A large stove, opposite, served for heat, cooking, and drying damp shoes in small niches. A built-in bench along one side furnished a warm seat. Drivers could take a nap on the polaty, a curtained platform fixed between the stove and ceiling.

∎

Overleaf: *The family ate and the parents slept in the same room. Behind the drapes the bed is layered with pillows, quilts, and a bobbin-lace trimmed coverlet.*

Page 44: *A glimpse of Dunya's room can be seen past a country armoire, made with axe and knife,* top. *The pictures are of Pushkin's characters. The master's desk is surrounded with trunks and suitcases,* bottom.

∎

Page 45: *A simple pine table and benches, rag runners, and icons furnish the drivers' room. The table stands across from the stove where water always simmered for the samovar.*

∎

TSIOLKOVSKY

A POOR GRADE-SCHOOL INSTRUCTOR named Konstantin Tsiolkovsky, considered by his neighbors to inhabit a world largely of his own invention, lived in this simple dwelling from 1904 until his death in 1935. Only later were his discoveries in the field of aerodynamics ratified and justly attributed. In honor of her father's contributions to the sciences that led to the Soviet conquest of space, Tsiolkovsky's sole surviving daughter was invited to the launch of Sputnik, the first Soviet satellite.

On a teacher's salary, Tsiolkovsky raised seven daughters in this modest wooden house in the town of Kaluga. Using his own carpentry skills, he divided the open area of the main floor into bedrooms for his children and converted a tiny space under the stairs into a kitchen. The scientist monopolized the second floor of the house with the workroom and study in which he also slept. His wife's bed was relegated to an upstairs landing.

Tsiolkovsky was a self-educated man with no university degree. In this house he modeled wood shapes to test them for aerodynamic properties, created wood turnings to explore textures for airborne machines, and every night crawled onto the roof with his telescopes to gaze at the heavens.

Tsiolkovsky's study was lit by a gas lamp rigged up to glide across the room on a stretched wire, opposite top. *His telescopes and papers sit about the room. On the desk lays the horn he used as a hearing device to counteract the deafness he suffered since childhood. One of his children's rooms is seen,* opposite bottom. *Each contained essentials attractively arranged.*

■

Overleaf: *The scientist's workshop contains the simple machines he devised to test his theories.*

He created turned-wood aerodynamic shapes at the workbench, and used a Lading's Jar fashioned from wine bottles to create electricity. Through this room he exited each night to sit on the porch roof with his telescopes.

■

VILLAGE HOUSES

THE TRADITION OF CREATING APPLIED architectural ornament in wood is carried forward today in innumerable small villages along Russian roadways. People in some provincial settlements take great pride in exhibiting their ability to carve intricate window frames, doorways, roof trim, and gates. These are the nineteenth- and twentieth-century *izba*s, or "wood houses," many without indoor plumbing, of the traditionally agrarian Russian people.

Houses are washed in bright color with contrasting lacy trim, largely in the only shades of paint available at the time the work was done. Small plots of land afford people the chance to grow their own vegetables and plant a few flowers to further brighten their homes.

Diminutive farmstands have sprung up in the last few years and have begun to recall the spirit of open commerce and the marketplace community for inhabitants of small towns. In roadside villages, peasants may now set out baskets of produce on the odd weathered-wood chair or old stool in front of their houses, in the hopes of attracting motorists eager for fresh, homegrown fare.

In Suzdal women set up stands to sell their produce in a village square, left. The scallop trim of the fence behind them, the painted overhead canopies, and an izba, or "wood house," seen in the distance show that decoration adds pattern and texture to even the simplest settings.

Elsewhere in town, a rain spout of a house is crowned with an urn sprouting a fantasy flower of tin, opposite. Vivid colors are used to highlight such special effects and to give the lacy woodwork its characteristic look.

■

*T*his house stands out among its neighbors as a small masterpiece of handwork, executed in painted wood and tin by its owner, Mr. Tolbien, above and opposite. Animal motifs across the façade celebrate his vocation as a farmer and avocation as a hunter. The trim was painted in as many colors as he could get his hands on.

The sun, a traditional vernacular symbol of the power of light over darkness, smiles beneficently on sections of the picket fence, top left. Large panels on an outbuilding portray a horse at three times of day: early morning, midday, and evening, top right.

■

Page 54: *The owner of this house in a roadside*

village created a herringbone pattern of paneling for its façade and chose to leave it in natural tones, the better to show off his expertise in woodworking. Decorative work painted white is undoubtedly an allusion to Russian lace.

■

Page 55: *A medley of windows shows the infinite variety of decorative*

trim applied to provincial wood houses. The oldest one here is remarkably elaborate, but monochromatic. Some houses still inhabited today are constructed of interlocked logs, joined by traditional methods. Others have board and batten façades that cover either logs or wood-frame construction.

■

CHAPTER 2

IMPERIAL PALACES

IMPERIAL PALACES

WHEN PETER THE GREAT AS-cended the throne in 1689, Russia was a backward country, still medieval in its culture. Peter transformed the nation into a major European power, in the process stifling many deeply held traditions of Muscovite society. In St. Petersburg he created a new, European-style capital that changed the face of Russia. Western observers quickly heralded the familiar classical style of the city's new buildings and proclaimed the birth of a "true" architecture in Russia, having considered the existing native ornamental style unworthy of that title. St. Petersburg's graceful buildings and broad avenues caused them to concede that Russia was no longer the uncivilized, barbarous nation its early, eclectic buildings had suggested.

Classicism appeared suddenly in Russia, after the movement had already gained favor abroad. The first examples of this new style were not entirely free of baroque and rococo elements, however, and betrayed the Russian delight in ornamentation. Because classicism was imported from Europe, many of St. Petersburg's great palaces were designed by foreign architects. One of the most prominent, the Italian-born Bartolomeo Rastrelli, combined standard classical features with elements of the ornate Muscovite style to create such lavish residences as the Winter Palace and the czar's summer residence, Peterhof. But

as the eighteenth century progressed, Russian classicism became increasingly strict, reaching its most conventional expression under Catherine the Great.

The sometimes excessive embellishments of the early palaces and estate houses were offset by their carefully planned formal gardens. In contrast to the lavishness of the buildings, the palace or estate grounds seemed sedate and orderly, and the symmetry that classicism brought to bear on the chaotic native elements in Russian design was most apparent in these gardens. While peasant villages continued to grow in haphazard fashion, the estates of the royalty and nobility bespoke rationality and logic.

The estate was an important part of Russian eighteenth-century life, influencing both the economy and the social consciousness of the nation. From the second half of the eighteenth century until well into the nineteenth, estates flourished throughout European Russia. But by the 1830s, such large households, often dependent on thousands of serfs, were no longer economically viable. By the time the serfs were liberated in 1861, the country estate was already a thing of the past. The finale to Chekhov's play *The Cherry Orchard* conveys this end of an era as the sound of axes chopping down trees is heard offstage.

Whether the estate belonged to royalty, nobility, or the landed gentry, it was ration-

ally planned with an eye for the ensemble, the way interior and exterior spaces worked together. A formal entranceway marked by an arch or pylons greeted the visitor and served to define the property line. The plantings were painstakingly laid out in appealing patterns, with statues depicting figures from history or mythology placed along the paths. Often the statuary was intended to teach about the past or offer allegories for the present. Similarly, the many pavilions, bridges, and gazebos were given instructive names to guide their use. A small pavilion called "Grotto" offered a place of meditation, while "Hermitage" promised solitude. With its opportunities for enjoyment and edification, the estate symbolized a deliberate way of life.

Even as the exurban palaces and estates provided a retreat from city life, they proved perfect places for extravagant entertainment. Estate owners organized elaborate festivals for hundreds of guests, with such bucolic pleasures as boating and strolling in summer, wildfowl and game hunting in autumn, and *troika* riding in winter. The houses were usually spacious enough to accommodate many people for many days, but feeding and sheltering so many in appropriate style would have been impossible without a large and servile staff.

As fashion changed in Russia, the strict classicism of the early gardens gave way to a romantic cult that idealized nature, which came to be reflected in the layout of the estate. A formal garden continued to serve as liaison between the house and the newly fashionable natural park or forest, where one could immerse oneself in nature. Significantly, even with the changes, a balance between house and grounds was always maintained. Thus, the somewhat baroque house or palace of the early eighteenth century worked surprisingly well with the highly formal gardens surrounding it while the more strictly classical domestic architecture of Empress Catherine II's reign, during the late eighteenth century, worked harmoniously with wilder gardens. In the ensemble of the estate, a softening of lines, a distortion of the absolute symmetry of the European model nearly always occurred, very much in keeping with traditional Russian taste. Also perceptibly Russian was the sense of whimsy and playfulness evident in the layout, statuary, and trick fountains of many parks. One of the overall aims of the estate was to surprise and enchant visitors, not just impress them.

The focal point of the estate remained the palace or manor house. Most estates were developed on the site of a decrepit or abandoned wooden house, which had commanded a lovely view. As in peasant architecture, the estate house rarely stood alone but rather constituted the dominant structure of an ensemble that included many subsidiary buildings. Such utility buildings as stables and barns were not attached to the main house as in peasant compounds, of course, but other pavilions and wings were connected by closed galleries or colonnades.

The center of attraction was a great hall for formal receptions and balls; around it were grouped smaller, more intimate drawing rooms. The large reception rooms had furniture placed against the walls so that people could mill about freely. In the drawing rooms, conversational groupings of settees and chairs were arranged in the corners. To make the central hall more dazzling, the walls were often faced in brilliant white marble or bleached linen. Drawing rooms were gentler, not intended to stimulate but to soothe, with the walls covered in pastel silks or other fabrics. The white and pastel wall coverings created a feeling of airiness which tempered the dreary climate, and large windows, often stretching from floor to ceiling, contributed to the brightness of the rooms.

Many of the important estates were designed by teams of Russian and foreign architects, and while European trends influenced their construction, the grand houses were not entirely divorced from the peasant aesthetic. For the copious gilding of the palaces was not simply an ostentatious display, but rather a keenly felt, atavistic attempt to capture the sun, its golden color changing with the time of day and the seasons, enhancing the beauty of the house. The house or palace itself was usually painted in a pastel shade that seemed luminous against the predominantly gray skies of northern Russia. In the nobles' houses the strong Russian feel for wood was evident in the elaborate parquetry of the flooring. Grains and rich colors were highlighted in intricate patterns combining such exotic and expensive woods as mahogany and rosewood with native birch and oak. In another combination of the im-

ported and the native, the great tile stoves heating—and sometimes merely decorating—virtually every room were not far removed from the masonry stoves of the peasant dwelling, though covered in Delft tile or marble. On the table the porcelain service might as easily be from Sèvres as from the Russian Imperial Porcelain Factory, while Bohemian cut crystal shared space with Russian niellowork vases.

Each palace was marked by the individuality of its owner and although one is initially bedazzled simply by the splendor of the three imperial summer residences standing today on the outskirts of Leningrad—Peterhof, Tsarskoe Selo, and Pavlovsk—personal taste is discernible. All three palaces were rebuilt after World War II, following their near total destruction. Fortunately, even in the chaos of impending siege, many valuable pieces had been sent to Siberia for safekeeping, and when evacuation of further pieces proved impossible, fabric swatches were saved and pictures taken. Thus, the restorations could be carried out faithfully on the basis of extensive documentation.

Peter the Great's Peterhof, the earliest summer palace, reflects the czar's love of the sea. The palace stands facing the Baltic Sea, at the very edge of the great Russian land mass. The sea and its somber colors frame the bright yellow building, as do its hundreds of canals and fountains. Many of these fountains are trick, capable of unexpectedly splashing the viewer. They culminate in the Grand Cascade, its seventy-five fountains descending seventeen terraced levels to join a canal that connects the palace to the sea. On its downward journey, the water plays off more than two hundred marble, bronze, and gilded lead statues, bas-reliefs, busts, and vases. This cascade unifies the entire estate, integrating promontory with lowland.

In contrast to the maritime spirit of Peterhof, both the Catherine Palace in Tsarskoe Selo (renamed Pushkin) and the palace at Pavlovsk are distinguished by more sylvan atmospheres. Until World War II, the Catherine Palace was surrounded by magnificent oaks; the Pavlovsk estate was known for its lush deciduous groves. Although both were imperial residences, the Catherine Palace was built with an eye to receptions and grand events, while the Grand Palace at Pavlovsk was designed as a private dwelling for Catherine the Great's son, Paul I.

It is expected that the czars had opulent dwellings, but the grandeur of some of the nobility's estates is surprising. Count Nikolai Sheremetyev's Ostankino is one such prosperous estate. Once situated on the outskirts of Moscow, it now sits right in the center of the city, overshadowed by a huge television tower. Inside the palace, however, the reality of contemporary life disappears amid the light-filled, lavishly gilded rooms. Like other estates, Ostankino was built on the site of an older wooden house. Stone construction replaced wood except in the main house, where wood was preferred for its better acoustic properties. Acoustics were at issue because Count

Sheremetyev conceived Ostankino as a theater-palace, unique among Russian estates. The count wanted a state-of-the-art stage for productions by his famous serf theater, which performed Russian and foreign operas, ballets, and comedies. The auditorium at Ostankino could seat over two hundred spectators, but its real innovation was that it could be converted into a ballroom within half an hour.

Ostankino's elaborate parquetry and carved portals, walls, pediments, and moldings testify to the highly skilled labor of Russian artisans, who possessed a special appreciation for the properties of wood. The large windows opening onto the grounds serve to integrate indoors and out, as do the numerous balconies, porches, and French doors. Like other eighteenth-century palaces, Ostankino represents a medley of styles derived from its owner and the Russian and foreign architects who designed it, as well as from the serfs who oversaw its construction.

All of the grand palaces and estates were nationalized following the 1917 Revolution. In an effort to convert the properties into museums, the government has spent billions of rubles on restoration, and attempts to re-create the opulence of the past have largely been successful. Even standing empty, the palaces and estate houses manage to impart a sense of a seductive and leisured—if self-indulgent—way of life, far removed from the pressures of the Soviet Union today.

PETERHOF

PETERHOF, OR PETRODVORETS, AS IT was renamed after the Second World War, embodies Peter the Great's grand plan for a summer residence on the banks of the Gulf of Finland. That the emperor gave it a German name (meaning "Peter's court") demonstrates his love of things European. In the decades after Peter's death, royalty continued to expand and improve on the compound of palaces, parks, fountains, and pavilions that make up the extensive complex.

The site was chosen first as a base of operations for the czar to oversee the construction of the nearby Kronstadt fortress, a stronghold against the invasion of his nascent capital at St. Petersburg. Later, a royal residence was planned in commemoration of the 1709 Russian victory over the Swedes, in which the empire won territory that ensured them an outlet to the Baltic Sea.

A palace on the breast of a hill overlooking the sea was conceived. But as its construction began,

Peter himself drew sketches for a more modest pavilion called Monplaisir, which could be built relatively quickly as a place for him to live while awaiting the completion of the palace and park ensemble. It turned out to be the emperor's favorite dwelling, and even after the more imposing palace was completed, he often chose to stay and entertain at Monplaisir.

Peter also called for the building of a romantic dining pavilion in which to hold intimate dinner parties by the sea. But the czar did not live to see the completion of the charming Hermitage in 1725. A century later, Nicholas I conceived of his own romantic getaway in an adjoining park, a neo-Gothic country house for himself and his family, which he called the Cottage. Among the many other structures at Peterhof, these three—Monplaisir, the Hermitage, and the Cottage—stand out as the most interesting and diverse.

The Samson Fountain, left, was named for the victory over the Swedes on St. Samson's Day in 1709 which gave the Russians access to the Baltic Sea. The basin of gilded statues sits at the end of the Grand Cascade and flows into the Marine Canal, which served as a water avenue to the sea. The canal was the official entrance to the grounds, and could float 115 vessels at a time.

■

In Peter the Great's time, many of the statues in the park's numerous fountains were made of ungilded iron. Their subsequent gilding proved effective as the golden surfaces seen through sprays of water enhance the play of light, opposite.

66

From the top of the Grand Cascade, the Marly Palace, named for a French royal residence, is seen in the distance. Water basins surround the pavilion, used as a guest cottage, giving it the appearance that it is floating. The formality of the overall plan of Petrodvorets is apparent from this vantage point.

MONPLAISIR

PETER THE GREAT RENDERED THE rough drawings for both the diminutive Monplaisir palace and its gardens. Under the direction of the German architect Johann Friedrich Braunstein, this charming brick residence took shape in the Dutch style on the shores of the Baltic Sea. Its main section was completed in 1716, after only two years of work.

The plan consisted of a single-story core of several rooms with flanking wings, light-filled arcades with French doors that opened on one side to flowers and on the other to the sea. Among the treasures of Monplaisir is a room that surrounds visitors with the beauty of a Russian lacquered box. In the galleries, studies, and ceremonial hall the czar displayed his oil paintings by Dutch and Flemish artists, acquired at auction in Amsterdam. The French artist Phillipe Pillement painted the spectacular ceilings throughout.

A terrace and balustrade extend out to the Baltic Sea on the north side of Monplaisir, right. Doors from one of the galleries open directly onto the terrace, above, bringing the water into view. The close relationship of Peter the Great's favorite residence to the Baltic reflects the czar's lifelong maritime passion.

Pages 68 and 69: *The architect Braunstein designed this small room of Chinese exotica for Peter I and a team of Russian icon painters led by a Dutch master executed the ninety-four panels set off by carved gilt and red lacquer. Ornamental brackets carry Chinese porcelains to the full height of the room.*

PETERHOF

*T*he Ceremonial Hall is the largest of Monplaisir's rooms. Its vaulted ceiling was painted by Phillipe Pillement to symbolize the four basic elements in the form of Greek gods. Among the canvases, five Dutch nautical scenes were judged to be of such accuracy by the czar that he used them to examine naval academy students.

72

This room, above left, was used by the emperor's personal secretary. Twenty-four paintings from Peter's collection are hung on the oak-paneled walls with crimson ribbon, as originally suspended. The emperor's room, above right, contains a replica of his canopy bed and seventeenth-century Spanish washstand.

■

Tiles from Delft cover the walls of the service kitchen, opposite. Cooking was done in an adjacent pavilion as a precaution against fire. English pewter and Dutch and Chinese porcelain were used at table.

HERMITAGE

THE NOTION OF INVITING A SMALL group of people to dine in a handsomely appointed pavilion placed in a natural setting was fashionable in eighteenth-century Europe. Having observed such novelties in his travels, Peter the Great re-created the effect at home, and even went the Europeans one better by designing two unique systems to add to the dining experience of his guests. The architectural plans of Johann Friedrich Braunstein called for a two-story structure. Inside, a pulley system was rigged to lower and raise the center of the table and/or individual plates, dumbwaiter style. In this way a party was never disturbed by hovering servants. The other of Peter's inventions drew his guests up to the second-floor dining room in an elevator chair for two.

74

The stucco façade of the Hermitage is heavily but elegantly adorned with white pilasters and trim, right. Guests crossed a moat by drawbridge to go to dinner.

■

Servants remained on the ground floor, where the kitchen and pantry were located. The crockery and serving pieces are eighteenth-century replacements of originals that were taken during World War II, above.

The wonderfully light and airy second-floor dining room opens all around to vistas of the sea and park, opposite.

The walls are covered from the chair rail to the ceiling by 124 European oil paintings, delineated by thin strips of gilded

wood. The cobalt-and-white china is Delft; the goblets and decanters from the Imperial Works in St. Petersburg.

■

Overleaf: *Adjacent to the Marly Palace is the Venus Park. The dikes that retain the Gulf of Finland here are fronted by a wall whose scalloped form creates bays that have been planted with espaliered trees. On top of the dike, clipped trees line a footpath and complete the fanciful effect.*

THE COTTAGE

IN THE ALEXANDRIA PARK, AMID GREEN meadows and stands of shade trees, are several buildings of smaller scale and less formal nature than other palaces at Peterhof. Among them is one whose yellow body with white trim appears as delectable as a three-layer cake. Cornices and fretwork drip down like icing from its steeply gabled roof and projecting verandas.

Dubbed the Cottage by Nicholas I, the house was built in 1826–29 for the czar's wife, Alexandra, for whom the park was named. Its design, in the neo-Gothic style then in vogue, was planned by the Englishman Adam Menelaws. In 1842 the dining room was expanded by Andrey Stakenschneider to meet the needs of the royal family. The Cottage is remarkable for the harmony of its interior and its human scale. The rooms reflect its frequent use as a family summer home.

A handsome collection of portrait miniatures, by European and Russian artists, are hung parallel to the window frames in the emperor's study, below. *The bust of Nicholas I is by I. Vitali.*

■

A bay window, above, *is capped with stained glass, a popular motif lifted from medieval castles. The vases are of nineteenth-century Russian cobalt or milk glass.*

■

The dining room's high-backed Gothic chairs and 5,200-piece set of porcelain and crystal from the Imperial Works in St. Petersburg are consistent with the overall stylistic theme, opposite. *All the fittings carry the blue coat of arms of Alexandra. For grand dinners, the crystal chandelier sparkled with thirty-six candles above a table set for twenty-four guests.*

■

The main drawing room occupies the central position on the first floor, opposite. The marvelous tracery of the plaster ceiling is complemented by a handwoven carpet incorporating Gothic rose window motifs. Fresh white roses were arranged in the room in honor of Alexandra, whose pet name as a child was "White Flower."

■

The two drawing-room fireplaces are each appointed with a nineteenth-century clock in the shape of a French Gothic cathedral. One can be seen, above left. Beyond the dining chairs, above right, uranium glass service pieces catch the light.

*N*icholas's dressing room, above, *has an oversize washstand of ash and marble by the cabinetmaker Heinrich Gambs. Lithographs depict battle scenes of the Russo-Turkish War of 1828–29. Concealed in one corner of the room is a spiral staircase by means of which ministers* ascended to the czar's study to deliver the morning reports.

■

The emperor's study is all of a piece in the Gothic style, opposite. Under his orders, the oak chairs were made in 1840 from trees, felled by a storm, that had originally been planted by Peter the Great *in his Summer Garden in St. Petersburg. Seventeenth- and eighteenth-century marine paintings hang in matching frames. The busts are of Nicholas's children.*

■

*Overleaf: Perched on the uppermost floor of the house is Nicholas's pri-*vate Marine Study, with *a view of the sea. His telescopes, compass, and silver megaphone remain on the desk. From here it was possible to supervise naval maneuvers between Kronstadt and St. Petersburg, using an optical telegraph. The walls and ceiling show beautiful trompe l'oeil work.*

MENSHIKOV

AIDING PETER THE GREAT IN ALL AS-
pects of planning and managing the new capital in
St. Petersburg was his close friend and the city's
first governor general, Prince Aleksandr Danilo-
vich Menshikov. His was one of the first stone
palaces erected in the city and surely the finest of
its day. Built in 1710–11, it remains the best example of the life-style of the early-eighteenth-century
nobility in St. Petersburg. Because it was frequented by the czar and his family, it also reveals
something of how the court functioned.

The construction of Menshikov's mansion was
overseen by the German architect Gottfried Scha-
del, who modeled it after late-seventeenth-century
European noblemen's dwellings. The politically
astute governor incorporated many of the European fashions that were not only permitted at the
time, but encouraged by the opinionated emperor.
The palace's decorative rooms, with their light
walls and large windows, were symbolic of the
new, Western value placed on comfort.

An eclectic mix of European furnishings bespoke the worldliness of the owner. Dutch tiles
were used in a stylish French manner to panel
entire rooms, creating "porcelain boxes" of some of
the suites. Mirrors—heretofore prohibited by
orthodox religion—were liberally hung about.
The governor's bedroom was arranged so that he
could receive important emissaries there, as in the
grand homes of French monarchs.

Menshikov's approach by boat, or that of any
important visitor, was heralded by a small orches-
tra that struck up a tune from the front balcony.
On special occasions luncheon parties easily
stretched into dinners, with teams of servants
changing table service and linens several times in
the course of a day of setting out fresh feasts.
Menshikov regularly hosted official events at this
house, allowing the czar full freedom to observe
guests' decorum and eavesdrop on court intrigues.

86

The carved and gilded jewel-encrusted box, right, is eighteenth-century Russian.

∎

As part of the European-ization of the decor, mar-ble statues were imported from Italy. In the fore-ground of the entrance hall, opposite, *stands a Roman Apollo from the*

second century A.D. The ground-floor hall led visitors straight through from the river dock to the courtyard for outdoor functions or up a grand staircase to the main ban-quet room. The delicate color and elaborate vaulting demonstrated the governor's apprecia-tion of European finery.

*T*he ochre exterior of Menshikov's palace is seen from the rear courtyard, *above left. Alterations and extensions of the palace's original plan continued until Menshikov's fall from power and exile in 1727. Pilasters with carved limestone capitals were* an innovative, exotic treatment for the original façade.

■

There are 27,810 unique, hand-painted tiles in the palace. A corner, above right, *shows how iron studs covered by gilt rosettes secured the ceiling work. Tilework was* not only beautiful but hygienic, an improvement on leather- or linen-covered walls, which invited dust and insects. The faience stove is eighteenth-century Russian.

■

On a wall of Menshikov's bedroom hangs a seventeenth-century tapestry, opposite. *An unusual cup made from a shell with a silver mount sits atop a small cabinet and was used by the emperor while traveling. A pair of chairs is covered with embossed leather upholstery. All are of European origin.*

*T*he bedroom on these pages is a reconstruction in the original style of such rooms in the palace. The German walnut bedstead and Flemish tapestry, above left, are probably from the seventeenth century. The eighteenth-century Turkish coverlet is woven of cotton, silk, and silver threads.

The late-seventeenth-century German dressing table service, above right, is made of solid silver. A detail of the bedside table, opposite, shows the rich medley of pattern and texture that grew out of combining fittings from various parts of Europe.

■

Page 92: A washstand similar to this seventeenth-century Swiss one was thought to be among the appointments in Menshikov's bedchamber. The Chinese enamel ewer and basin are of the same period. Page 93: The Walnut Study was paneled in natural wood in 1717, a rare treatment in Russia. It was the favorite room not only of the

owner, but of Peter the Great, who made use of it during his visits. The Dutch cabinet is of tortoise shell and wood; the eighteenth-century Italian chairs, of gilded walnut. The portrait of the czar is by the Dutch painter Jan Weenix, from the late seventeenth century.

■

TSARSKOE SELO

IF PETERHOF WAS PETER THE GREAT'S Versailles, then the Catherine Palace at Tsarskoe Selo (now Pushkin) was Empress Elizabeth's. The second daughter of Peter I, she inherited not only his title but his love of grandeur and his desire to express it through westernized architecture. Fortunately, the spirited czarina chose an architect of great talent to interpret her wishes: Bartolomeo Francesco Rastrelli. His creations, which include the Winter Palace (now the Hermitage museum), were to define what many have come to think of as imperial Russian style.

By 1752, Rastrelli had begun work on the most opulent and lasting version of the summer palace started under Elizabeth's mother, Catherine I, for whom the palace was named. The completed structure integrated the previous building and its modifications into a mammoth thousand-foot-long edifice encrusted with pillars and capitals, vases and garlands, sculptures and balustrades. The fa-

çade was originally painted clear yellow and all the reliefwork was gilded. Golden domes punctuated a gleaming roof made of silvery sheet iron. The finished extravagance was breathtaking to some, blindingly gaudy to others. Given the requirements of his commission, Rastrelli had produced one of the most exuberant expressions of Russian baroque—that curious hybrid of curvaceous European line with extravagant Russian scale and color.

The gleam of the exterior was echoed by miles of carved giltwork inside. In spite of the grandiosity of the golden interior, the device of cutting the palace's length into interconnected smaller reception rooms gave the rooms a surprisingly human scale. The grand finale of the elongated plan was the Great Hall, a room over a thousand yards square in which windows alternate with three hundred mirrors to augment the glitter.

The Golden Gallery, a series of ornately framed doorways that open the full length of the structure, connects all the state rooms, right. With doors ajar, the gallery artfully forces perspective of the elongated space.

∎

Elizabeth's portrait, opposite, painted by a Ger-

man artist, hangs in one room, its frame awaiting regilding. Fourteen thousand Russians are said to have worked to restore the palace since it was all but destroyed in World War II.

∎

Page 96: *A window detail from a side extension of the main façade shows*

uncharacteristic restraint and charming detail. Page 97: *In 1860, the main staircase area was redone in rococo style by Ipolit Monigetti. Here, a section of its carved plaster walls and an embedded barometer that features the heavens.*

∎

*T*he Cavaliers' Dining Room, opposite, was a setting for state dinners. The table takes its form from the Cyrillic letter E (for Empress Elizabeth) and is set with porcelain from the famous Gardner factory. The faience stoves here and elsewhere were only decorative, as the palace was used as a summer residence.

Elizabeth bought a collection of 135 French, Dutch, and Italian canvases in Prague in 1747 to cover the walls of this reception room, top left. A uniquely Russian method of hanging them results in the look of extravagant wall covering. In the rococo main hallway, lower right, plasterwork supports a complement of eighteenth-century Japanese and Chinese porcelains.

■

A portion of the gate, top right, shows the imperial double-headed eagle. Because of its enormity, the palace is best seen a portion at a time, lower left. Catherine the Great actually toned down the façade by removing much of the giltwork and painting it blue.

Overleaf: The Great Hall was designed by Rastrelli. Seven-hundred candles in wall sconces illuminated the room for the balls and masquerades of which Elizabeth was so fond. The palace was electrified early, in the late nineteenth century, to lessen the possibility of fire. This room took twenty years to restore.

PAVLOVSK

THE SUMMER HOME BUILT AND NAMED for the future emperor Paul I is the epitome of the imperial classical style. Its overall harmony is all the more remarkable considering that the edifice was labored over by more architects than any other royal residence. Not only did they accomplish significant work here, but each managed to add to the contributions of his predecessors without greatly disturbing what had already been accomplished. The cornerstone of the Grand Palace was laid in 1782, but it was nearly fifty years before the ensemble was finished.

The site was earlier a royal hunting ground, chosen in part for its proximity to Tsarskoe Selo. Bequeathed by Catherine the Great to her son Paul on the birth of his first son, the property was given to her favorite architect, the gifted Scotsman Charles Cameron, to design. He drew plans for the main palace and for much of the park. His designs and those of his successor Vincenzo Brenna were quite complete, to the extent that they also planned the interiors. In 1800 Giacomo Quarenghi was asked to design five new rooms. He was followed by Andrey Voronikhin, who restored areas destroyed by fire in 1803. Carlo Rossi added to the palace in 1816 and again in 1822–24.

Pavlovsk reflects the veneration of European classicism and the architectural restraint made fashionable by Catherine the Great and taken up by Paul and his wife, Maria Fyodorovna. Known for her good taste and appreciation of the arts, Maria had much to do with the final look of the palace. She outlived her husband by more than a quarter of a century and continued to make additions and modifications to the palace after his assasination in 1801. Pavlovsk remained her home until her death in 1828.

The site's gently rolling hills, forests, and meandering river were beautifully exploited by Charles Cameron. Pavlovsk presides over the Slavyanka River, left. Integrated with nature, as few of the Russian palaces are, the elegant, square main section features a simple colonnade and pediment. Its side wings were an addition by Vincenzo Brenna.

The Temple of Friendship, opposite, was so named in honor of the eighteenth-century ideal of love. For the pavilion, Cameron designed a rotunda with sixteen columns and a flat dome that is both monumental and graceful. Bas-relief medallions illustrate the main themes of both platonic and romantic love.

■

*P*aul and Maria Fyodorovna maintained separate private rooms in the palace. The empress's study held her remarkable desk chair/cachepot designed by Andrey Voronikhin, above left. The tapestries are Gobelin, and the marble statues are eighteenth-century Italian replicas of Roman originals.

The porphyry collection, above right, was brought back by Paul and Maria from their European travels for the anteroom to Maria's boudoir. The porcelain top and legs for the bronze-framed table were made at the Imperial Works in St. Petersburg. The table depicts the original palace as designed by Cameron.

The strictly classical theme of the Grecian Hall is carried through, opposite, in one of two large jasper urns with finely engraved bronze heads at the handle bases, designed by Voronikhin. These urns are considered to be among the best examples of early-nineteenth-century Russian stone carving.

Page 106: The form of Paul's dressing room was Cameron's work, the beautiful trompe l'oeil painting, Brenna's. The room's elegant, subtle colors and oval shape set it apart from most imperial apartments. Page 107: The exceptional Grand Vestibule was worked on by the palace's first three architects.

Maria's corner sitting room, opposite, was designed by Carlo Rossi in 1816 to accommodate intimate gatherings of the poets, writers, and composers of whom she was so fond. The walls are lavender polished faux marbre.

The furniture is birch, of Rossi's design.

∎

The canopy of Empress Maria's bed can be glimpsed in the mirror's reflection, above left. The extraordinary decorative work of her state bedroom includes painted silk hangings, a carved four-poster bed by Henri Jacob of Paris, and a marble fireplace inlaid with malachite. This ceremonial room was modeled after that of French royalty and was never actually slept in by the empress.

A sumptuous vase made at the Ludwigsburg porcelain works in Germany incorporates portraits of Paul and Maria, above right. The piece was presented to the couple by Maria's uncle, the duke of Württemberg and owner of the factory.

*T*he Grecian Hall is a grand ballroom designed by Cameron and meant to recall a classical temple, opposite and above. Sixteen green Corinthian columns of faux *marbre* support an entablature ornamented with garlands. The carved ceiling and frieze add to the room's rich texture. The plaster statues are replicas of Greek originals.

■

Brenna and Voronikhin contributed to the interior of the Grecian Hall. Its grace and unity are noteworthy considering the input of three diverse architects. This chair, above, is from a suite of four divans and twenty-two chairs of painted and gilded wood, designed by Voronikhin and made in St. Petersburg for the palace's restoration after its 1803 fire.

■

OSTANKINO

THE PALACE AT OSTANKINO IS AN OUT-standing example of eighteenth-century architecture, interior design, art, and landscaping—all accomplished by master serfs. It survived Napoleon's invasion of Moscow in 1812 more or less intact and its location on the outskirts of Moscow placed it far from the thrust of the German troops, which all but destroyed other such precious estates in the environs of Leningrad during World War II. Its current restoration was begun in 1918.

The property had been in the hands of boyars since at least the sixteenth-century and had even belonged to Ivan the Terrible at one time. The present palace was built in 1795 by Count Nikolai Sheremetyev. At that time, the thirty-six-year-old nobleman's holdings included over two million acres spread over seventeen provinces with more than two hundred thousand serfs. He was as well educated as he was well-heeled, and his support of culture culminated in the construction of his private palace of the arts at Ostankino. He commissioned a team of architects to plan an edifice that included art galleries and a theater to complement a dramatic and diverse series of reception rooms, calculated to tease the eye as well as to circulate his guests at grand functions. The celebrated Argunov family—serf artists bound to Sheremetyev—spearheaded the execution of the interior work.

Here Count Sheremetyev and his family passed idle summer days and entertained on such state occasions as when Ostankino hosted Emperor Paul I and his entourage after the emperor's coronation. For this event, the road from Moscow to Ostankino was illuminated with flaming arches and torches. At the emperor's approach a whole avenue of trees, readied earlier, was toppled to either side, opening up a grand vista of the palace and a memorable fireworks display.

A Dancing Faun, left, stands along each of the side galleries that form the main courtyard.

■

The four columns in the backstage of the theater, opposite, served as support, while sixteen decorative side columns were made of pasteboard and could be pushed back against the walls during plays. After a performance the theater could be converted into a ballroom in less than an hour. Its ceiling was painted by artist Ivan Serzhantsev.

■

Overleaf: *To offset the grand scale of the rooms in the main palace, the Italian Pavilion in a side wing was carefully planned for more intimate receptions. A detail shows the intricacy of decorative effects which took precedence over majestic architectural gestures in these rooms. The flowered wall covering, imported from France, is the only example of such paper from the eighteenth century to survive in Russia. The Roman marble head of Aphrodite is from the first century A.D. and is the oldest piece in the palace. The chair is Russian from the late eighteenth century.*

■

*I*n the Blue Room, op-posite, *one of the most delicately appointed galleries, decorative work executed by serfs reaches an apex with immaculately carved and gilded wooden torchères that each hold seventeen candles, made under the direction of Ivan Mochalin. Such elaborate chande-liers in this and the Crimson Room (through doorway) were supplemented by multitudes of sconces and girandoles. Marble Atlantes support a door entablature of fashionable Egyptian motifs. A matching aqua brocade was used for draperies, on walls, and as upholstery.*

An indoor loggia, above right, was designed by Italian Giacomo Quarenghi with three graceful bays defined by faux marbre *columns. The furniture is French by Paul Spol. The portrait is of Alexander I.*

■

The central six-column portico of the pal-ace is seen beyond an eighteenth-century Italian statue of Apollo Belvedere, above left. The exterior's pale rose-and-white scheme supports the cool classic symmetry of the structure. The palace is a masterpiece of deception: what appears as masonry is actually wood frame covered with stucco.

*R*ichly carved and glazed doors open into the Italian Pavilion, above left. *Beyond, one of the four small rooms into which the wing is divided. A corner room in the main palace, above right, with damask walls, carved door frames, and an Italian marble bust.*

The walls of the Art Gallery, opposite, are of a bold blue that has come to be strongly associated with Russian residential architecture. Original oils by Rubens, Rembrandt, and Titian were looted by Napoleon's troops. Serf artists executed the painted ceiling. The parquet is by Taude and the chandelier by Fischer, both of St. Petersburg.

■

Overleaf: *The Crimson Room glows like a gem with garnet-colored, velvet upholstered walls. The grace of a trio of Russian marble amphorae* belies their true weight. The chairs and marble-topped tables are gilded. Throughout, the brave use of color distinguishes this palace from its European counterparts.

■

YUSUPOV

DURING THE NINETEENTH CENTURY, this Petersburg palace housed several generations of one of Russia's families of longstanding influence. Prince Dimitri Yusupov had been an advisor to Peter the Great. His grandson became one of Empress Elizabeth's favorites. Prince Nikolai Yusupov, the owner of the house, worked his way into Catherine the Great's inner circle. Later he became a confident of Emperor Paul and tutor to his sons, the future czars Alexander I and Nicholas I. It was Nikolai's grandson Felix Felixovich who in 1916 poisoned the supremely powerful Grigori Rasputin in a basement room of the palace to which the victim was led through a mirrored trick passage. With his co-conspirators, the young Yusupov finished off the murderous job by means of an axe, gunfire, and drowning.

The mansion, built on the banks of the Moika Canal by the architect de la Motte in 1760, was purchased by Prince Nikolai Yusupov in the early 1800s. As the family home of a man of rank, it contained a special entry for carriages, several reception rooms, a billiards room, a grand picture gallery, concert hall, and theater.

One spectacular room was designed in the fashionable Moorish style by the Italian architect Ipolit Monigetti. With an onyx fireplace, inlaid marble floors, carved marble wall panels, and a working fountain with a basin made from a single stone, the effect was rather marvelous. In addition, virtually every surface—in stone or wood—was hand worked with a combination of rich color and gilt. Another room that remains perfectly intact from the nineteenth century is a theater built to accommodate two hundred persons. Elaborate gilding, which included the application of both green and yellow gold leaf, makes it shine like a jewel.

Although the Moorish room's furniture did not survive the Second World War, replacements have been made in the style of the originals, left. A grouping of diverse tables and stools in the Eastern spirit, some inlaid with mother-of-pearl.

One of two busts of Moors in painted marble placed on columns, opposite. The lower wall panels are made of marble, carved in a geometric design, and colored with wax. Small niches are of carved plaster seemingly supported by miniature marble columns.

*T*he Moorish room was designed by Italian architect Ipolit Monigetti with a series of arches that divide the space in two, above left. Quotes from the Koran are inscribed on some of the walls. The wooden doors seen here are original, but the chandelier is a replacement.

■

A colorful detail, above right, shows the intricacies of the carved and painted plasterwork where deep coffers enhance ceiling shadows. Changes of pattern were undertaken at every opportunity—for arches, edgings, borders, doorway frames, and capitals.

■

Still in use today, the Yusupov theater, opposite, retains many of its period fittings. The interior was rebuilt in the nineteenth century by a Russian architect named Stepanov. The chairs are original, as is the curtain painted by the artist Alexander Golovin.

CHAPTER 3

GOLDEN AGE

GOLDEN AGE

DESPITE THE SPLENDOR OF THEIR grand palaces and golden-domed churches, Russian cities of the nineteenth century were neither comfortable nor inviting. Each spring the unpaved streets became bogs through which pedestrians had to make their way gingerly along makeshift planks. Horses and carriages regularly sank into the mud and wallowed there. In the dry days of summer, the streets generated billows of dust and grime. Because most of the streets were unlit at night, it was often wiser to stay at home. As one contemporary remarked, "Both prudence and vanity promoted the virtues of domesticity."

Russian cities comprised not only palaces and tenements, but substantial houses built of wood and stone. A specific vocabulary identified the different types of dwellings. Most basic was the *dvor*, a wooden house more capacious than the *izba*, or "peasant cottage," but still distinctly modest, even rude. *Khoromy* described a larger house constructed of wood and closer to a mansion, while a house of similar size made of brick or stone and inhabited by a member of the nobility was called *palaty*, or "chambers." The now standard word for house, *dom*, was used for the masonry houses of prosperous merchants. Varied as these residences were, stylistically they all had much in common with the *izba*, built upon a half-story, sporting extravagant ornamentation, and laid out in the characteristic pattern of add-ons. Thus, despite their increased size and solidity, these houses relied more on traditional design than innovation.

With city land not yet at a premium, urban residents could enjoy spacious courtyards, gardens, and even orchards, as well as outbuildings such as steam baths and stables. As late as the 1870s, cows were still a common sight in Moscow. In the city as well as in the country households retained as many serfs as possible, from locksmiths to personal pastry chefs, to keep their daily lives running efficiently. Society judged a household's wealth by the number of "souls," or male serfs, it maintained (women workers did not count toward a family's wealth). A well-to-do family of average size might keep fifty serfs in the city and half again as many at their country home. Even after the serfs were emancipated in 1861, most stayed on as poorly paid servants.

Nineteenth-century Russian domestic architecture reflected the changing times—the decline of the great estates and the rise of the haute bourgeoisie, a group with heterogeneous tastes and money to support every whim. Their houses, from the understated to the lavish, are best described as eclectic. Not infrequently, the exterior architecture displayed such comic juxtapositions as neoclassical pillars alongside folk-style carvings. Indoors, a mingling of brocade and tulle signaled the uncertain marriage of East and West.

Above all, the nineteenth century was an era of burgeoning bourgeois comfort, manifested among the monied classes as a fascination with things European. This new commercial class, however, never entirely eschewed products of local manufacture. Typically, the proud homeowner reserved for himself and his immediate family the fancy carved chairs from French or German workshops, while relegating the more primitive benches assembled by the household staff to the poorer relations living in the house on charity.

Virtually every affluent resident of the city, even the struggling lesser gentry, kept a country house. Once the roads became passable in the summer, families made the pilgrimage to their *dacha,* staying throughout the autumn and its gala hunt season, and returning to town only at the onset of winter. Even then, sleigh rides and other winter diversions prompted outings to the country. The *dacha* was generally constructed of logs cased with planks, which were often painted in vivid colors. Inside, the boards were covered with plaster, yielding a much warmer design than plain stone or brick. One peculiarity of this construction, however, was the startling sound, like gunshots, caused by the shifting of the walls during heavy frosts.

The city residence was more formal than the *dacha.* For fire prevention, houses in the central part of the city were frequently built of brick, or if that proved too expensive, the lower floor was faced with brick while the upper story was wood. In their urban dwellings, the Russians at-

tempted to be more modern and European, whereas at the *dacha* they could indulge their Russian roots. This domestic split mirrors the larger societal rift that occurred between Westernizers and Slavophiles in the nineteenth century, typified by the characters of Oblonsky and Levin in Lev Tolstoy's *Anna Karenina.* Oblonsky chooses city life and French manners, while Levin remains very Russian in his attachment to the land, representing Tolstoy's own preference. Most members of the landed gentry, however, were unable to reconcile fully the different modes of life signified by the Western town house and the Russian country house, feeling eternally caught between the two.

All Russian families were preoccupied with keeping warm, and dwellings in both town and country were built for as much energy efficiency as possible. Rarely was heated space entered directly from the outdoors. Instead, one might step into all manner of closed porches, vestibules, anterooms, and passageways that served as buffers against the chill. A series of unheated corridors led to different areas of the house, conveniently linking larders and other storerooms with living space. The best-designed houses had two kitchens: a smaller winter kitchen nestled partly underground for insulation, and a summer one, apart from the main house so that the cooking heat would not cause discomfort.

For maximum efficiency within the house, large masonry stoves were placed on the walls between rooms so that a single stoking could heat both spaces and no heat escaped outdoors. A rambling country house might have ten or fifteen such stoves, which radiated heat for a good twelve hours between firings. The windows were also notable; in place of double glazing, the Russians used two sets of windows, the outer opening out, the inner pair opening in. The second set of windows was sealed in the winter and removed in the summer to allow fresh air to enter. For wintertime ventilation, a *fortochka,* a small window cut into both panes of glass, could be opened as desired to freshen the air without freezing it.

As for interior decoration, houses varied as much as their owners. The floors were usually finished in parquet patterns and either left bare in the Russian style or covered with carpets after the European fashion. Furniture boasted elaborate marquetry. Colored-glass chandeliers mirrored rich portieres shading doorways, while matching curtains, often draped in neoclassical swags, gave the rooms a shrouded, cozy look. Ceilings were sometimes painted with frescoes. But even in the most sophisticated houses, the Russian feel for wood remained evident in the decorative flooring and trim work.

In contrast to both the marbled walls of the palaces and the unfinished logs of the *izba,* the plaster walls of the bourgeois home were simply washed in hues of rose, blue, or green or else covered with fine bleached linen painted a pastel shade. Whereas palace stoves were encased in marble or imported Delft tile and peasant stoves were covered in stucco, the stoves of merchants and the gentry were usually faced with bright tiles of local fabrication. The bourgeoisie used metalware in place of the nobility's gold and porcelain and the peasantry's wood and birch bark, and were especially keen on ormolu, a kind of brass crafted to resemble gold, thus serving both economy and pretension.

One distinctive feature of the bourgeois Russian house lay in the sleeping arrangements. For all the elegance of the public rooms, Russians paid little attention to bedrooms, even though considerable numbers of guests, both permanent and temporary, were frequently in residence. Even at the highest levels of society, far from seeking refinement in their bedchambers, Russians slept anywhere they fell. Elaborately carved ornamental screens in the drawing rooms were all that shielded divans designed both for tête-à-tête conversations and sleeping, and all too often a groan or snore betrayed the presence of someone sleeping only a few feet away. This practice of masking private functions behind elegant public screens is perhaps quite telling about Russian nature.

The French author Théophile Gautier, who visited Russia in 1858, expressed some distaste for the furniture he saw in one particular residence—a huge polar bear stuffed for use as a sofa, with end tables fashioned from stuffed black bear cubs. He deemed more positive such features of the typical bourgeois home as the large round *zakuska,* or hors d'oeuvre table, always set for unexpected guests, and the heavy curtains and massive stoves that kept the rooms warm. Special racks by the stoves held visitors' fur coats, which absorbed enough warmth to keep the wearers toasty for one or two hours even in subzero temperatures. The stoves generated so much heat that Gautier likened Russian wintertime rooms to greenhouses. Indeed, fashion called for adorning the rooms with exotic houseplants as an antidote to the endless expanses of snowy white outside, and the ample heat in the rooms made it possible for women to dress in décolletage, otherwise unthinkable in such a harsh climate.

A wide range of styles can be seen in the houses—now museums—that once belonged to some of Russia's best writers and artists. The poet Alexander Pushkin enjoyed a courtly upbringing and cosmopolitan connections, and the furnishings of his rooms, with their French sensibility, bespeak elegance and refinement. In contrast, Lev Tolstoy consciously cultivated simplicity in his surroundings as in his life, even though closer scrutiny reveals expensive table settings and fine portraits on the walls hardly typical of peasant dwellings. Anton Chekhov and Fyodor Dostoevsky lived in less distinctive, urban apartments, though typically their rooms convey a sense of character amid the modest bourgeois comfort. Most inviting are the studies, with assorted bibelots providing a glimpse into the writers' private worlds. The decor of Chekhov's Moscow town house is conservative, as befits the doctor which he was, but his residence in the Crimea is brighter and more relaxed, in keeping with the southern temperament of the place.

In the first half of the nineteenth century, most houses displayed little of the old Russian style. However, in the 1870s, a wealthy industrialist established an artists' colony at Abramtsevo, which set about re-creating the Russian aesthetic of the Muscovite period that had been displaced by Peter the Great's reforms. The artists organized workshops in traditional crafts for the newly liberated serfs, to provide them a livelihood and to keep such artistry alive. The buildings and furnishings designed and made there represented a new nationalist style with their extensive ceramics and tile-work, ornate wood carvings, handwoven linens, painted utensils, and designs from mythology and folklore, and so brought about a Russian revival in architecture.

In addition to Russian revival, other architectural styles appeared at the turn of the century. The Ryabushinsky mansion where the writer Maxim Gorky lived is impressive not only in its bold art nouveau style, but also in its focus on detail: the house's commanding staircase, the beautifully crafted woodwork, hand-wrought window and door hardware, stained glass, and skylights. All show a concern for balancing the decorative with the practical.

Even in the Gorky house, which largely follows European style, the deep Russian desire to harmonize the man-made with the natural is apparent. In defining a code of comfort, the best nineteenth-century designers sought to bring poetry to daily life, just as the peasants did in their simple cottages. In contrast to the overt opulence of palaces and estates, Russian bourgeois houses aspired less to pretension than to charm and *gemütlichkeit*, manifesting the deeply held belief that beauty can perfect man and make him richer.

PUSHKIN

AMONG THE RUSSIAN PEOPLE, COUNT Alexander Sergeevich Pushkin is the most universally loved of all the great writers. Popularly, his distinction as the first celebrated poet of Russian literature is matched in notoriety by the tragic nature of his death. A duel took his life in 1837 at age thirty-eight and accorded him immediate martyr status. He fought with a French military officer for the honor of his wife, Natalya, reportedly the most beautiful woman in St. Petersburg. After several days of suffering, Pushkin died in the study of his apartment. For distraught admirers, the attending physician posted notices outside the door as the poet's condition worsened.

Pushkin's apartment is located on the Moika Canal in the heart of old St. Petersburg. He leased the rather grand flat in 1836 for his wife, their four children, and her two sisters but did not always manage to pay the rent. A fine yellow-and-white eighteenth-century façade concealed the cobbled inner courtyard and small garden. Light and airy, the place consisted of eleven rooms laid out in railroad fashion, each painted a different color. Today the furnishings are somewhat sparse as the creation of an accurate restoration has moved slowly.

The young poet's library housed about 4,500 books in fourteen languages. His study is a true workspace, noted by his contemporaries for its lack of pomp. It is filled with mementos, in addition to books, rather than with sculpture and showpieces. Among his effects is a portrait by the poet Vasily Zhukovsky, given to Pushkin on the publication of his first poem, and inscribed, "To the victorious pupil from the vanquished teacher."

134

The entrance to the courtyard of the neoclassical building where Pushkin lived in the years before his untimely death is seen, left. The elegant eighteenth-century building has two vaulted entry tunnels, a courtyard garden, and typical ironwork door canopies.

∎

In the parlor, opposite, a copy of a famous portrait of the poet hangs over a nineteenth-century settee similar to one that was in the room at the time he lived here.

*O*n Pushkin's desk, above, stands a blackamoor figure that reminded him of his great-grandfather who was taken as a boy from Ethiopia to be a servant for Peter the Great. Also seen are his papers and brass bell. Against the wall is a bayonet from a Russian battle with the Turks and a wooden coffer he called Hannibal's box, after his great-grandfather.

■

Stacks of Pushkin's unsold volumes remain on hallway shelves, opposite top. A corner of the study where the poet liked to sit and read, opposite bottom. A few of his collected walking sticks lean against the chair and shelves.

■

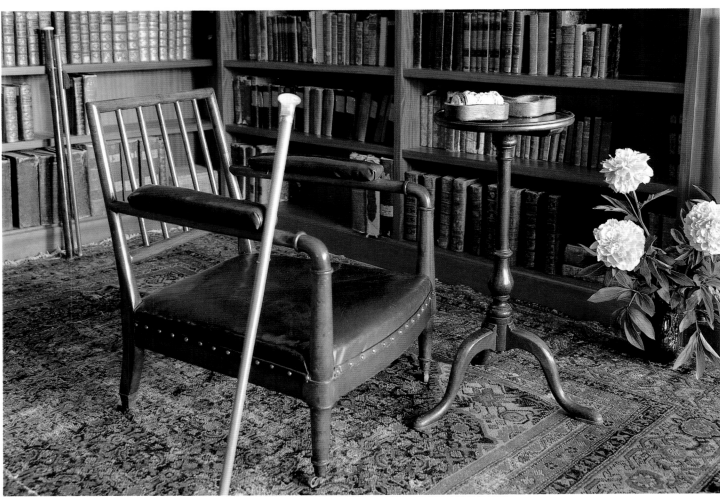

*H*ere and elsewhere in the apartment, girandoles, candelabra, and chandeliers are delicate examples of nineteenth-century Russian work, above left. The bedroom of one of Natalya's sisters was canary yellow, above right; the rooms' hues were chosen by the landlord. A tile woodburning stove intrudes minimally into the room. A piano stands across from the parlor's seating area, opposite.

■

TOLSTOY

YASNAYA POLYANA, THE ESTATE WHERE Lev Nikolaevich Tolstoy lived for fifty years, is one of the few intact relics of gentrified country life from the nineteenth century. It is among the most beautiful houses in Russia not only because it was decorated with excellent and, even rarer understated taste, but also because it is authentic in every detail to the period before the writer's death in 1910.

In the hands of Tolstoy's aristocratic family since the late seventeenth century, this once-active farm is located in the countryside outside the city of Tula. The name Yasnaya Polyana means "clear glade," and indeed, the homey white house that was enlarged by Tolstoy sits in a meadow surrounded by forests. The park consists of miles of well maintained wooded pathways, dappled birch allées, and ponds—places the writer liked to walk in solitude. The movingly simple green mound that is his grave is located in a nearby clearing by a stream.

Count Tolstoy returned here with his bride, Sofya Andreevna, in 1862 and wrote in his diary, "Immense happiness. . . . It is impossible that all this should end except with life itself." The great writer, in all things prolific, proceeded to father thirteen children by his wife and at least as many out of wedlock. At the estate, Tolstoy wrote *War and Peace* and *Anna Karenina*, and here he played out his agrarian/egalitarian theories. He became a vegetarian, worked the fields, and wore the simple tunics that still hang in his bedroom. The house is noteworthy for its lack of fuss, its simple beauty: no pattern-on-pattern here, no grand displays of collections. Light, air, and wood play strong roles in the interior of the house, resulting in an amiable marriage of dwelling to site.

A bit of the naive, carved porch railing shows through the vines, left. *One of the charms of the estate is its combination of purposefully simple fittings, locally made, with more sophisticated pieces.*

■

Opposite: *(counterclockwise from upper right)* *The house seen from a garden path; a birch bridge through a bog in the forest; the main drive; Tolstoy's grave. His younger brother said, "Happiness is to be found in the place of the green stick." By a stream in the woods, Tolstoy felt he had discovered that place. Here he is buried.*

Page 142: *A corner of Sofya's room has a settee and a wall of family photos. Women's bedrooms in the nineteenth century often had such a sitting area where intimate friends could visit. White slipcovers were generally in use in the summer and sometimes year-round.*

■

Page 143: *The dining room was large enough for the everyday use of the family of fifteen and for entertaining. The portrait of Sofya is by Valentin Serov, that of Lev is by Ilya Repin, under whom Serov studied. Austrian bentwood chairs and settees encircle several tables.*

Pages 144–45: *Tolstoy's bedroom is as he left it in 1910. The pillow was embroidered by his sister; the blanket under the coverlet, knitted by his wife. The portrait over the bed is of his eldest daughter, Tatiana, painted by her friend Iulia Igumnova.*

■

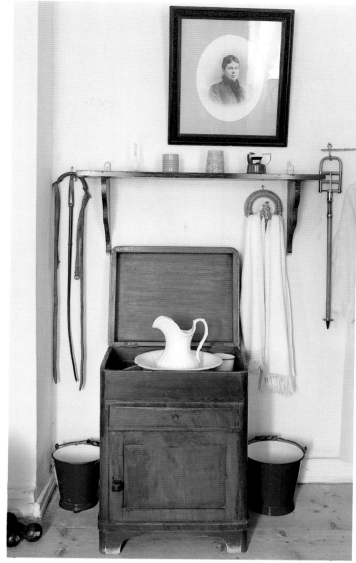

A room on the ground floor saw many uses, opposite top. Once it was for storage; later, Sofya stayed here during visits before her marriage; for a while, Tolstoy wrote and slept here; in 1910, his daughter was living in it as it is now furnished.

∎

Tolstoy's library contained some 22,000 books, over half in French or English. Some of the English volumes were kept in the entrance hall, opposite bottom. *A box of family tennis racquets was kept under the farm-made bench.*

∎

In the writer's study, above left, *the frame of the sofa/trundle bed was filled with manuscripts. A child's chair at the* desk was his remedy for myopia: seated in it he could be close to his work without using eyeglasses. *On the bookshelf are works of Thoreau, Emerson, Muhammad, and Gandhi. Photographs by Orlov of peasants in izbas hang over the sofa.*

∎

On one side of Tolstoy's bedroom hang his walking sticks and riding crop, above right. *Tolstoy arose each morning at seven o'clock, walked or exercised—near the washstand are his barbells—then joined his wife for tea. He wrote until one o'clock P.M., took lunch, and rested. In the evenings he resumed writing.*

∎

DOSTOEVSKY

THIS COZY APARTMENT BELONGED TO the Russian writer one most associates with darkness and despair—Fyodor Mikhailovich Dostoevsky. That his last years were spent in such comfort is due to his wife, who helped reverse his early misfortunes. The writer's near execution and eight-year exile to Siberia for subversion, a failed first marriage, a penchant for gambling, and a bankruptcy had all threatened to ruin him. Faced with a book contract and impossible deadline for *The Gambler,* he hired Anna Grigoryevna Snitkina, who became his dedicated secretary and then, following the book's publication, his wife.

Dostoevsky had a fixation for corner flats, of which this is one. He lived here from 1878 until 1881, when he died in his study while making an entry in his diary. Many of the settings have been faithfully reconstructed from photographs taken of the apartment or from drawings by family members. The warm rooms are furnished for the most part with typical nineteenth-century fittings. The writer loved to entertain friends and family and kept a big dining table and samovar at the ready. One of the nicest rooms is that of his children, still filled with their lessons, paint pots, and toys.

In this apartment he wrote *The Brothers Karamazov.* He often worked at night, preferably by candlelight, with pots of strong tea and cigarettes as his late night companions. His wife kept the children at bay, though they sometimes communicated by slipping notes under the door of his study. Among the papers that were found on his desk when he died was a note from his daughter: "Dear Papochka, I love you. Lyuba."

148

A doll and rocking horse stand near a woodburning stove, in the room of Lyuba and Fedi, Dostoevsky's daughter and son, left. The tragedy of his third child's death at the age of three had prompted the family's move to this apartment.

■

The entry, opposite, is the most sparsely appointed of the rooms: a place to remove coats and hats and spruce up before entering the drawing room. Yellow wallpaper in a cheery tile pattern is set off by dark-stained wood furniture of Russian origin. A stove warmed the space.

An oval wooden box that held the writer's tobacco and papers for rolling cigarettes has been preserved on the drawing room table, above left. On the underside of the box his daughter wrote, "28 January 1881. Today father died."

■

Patterned wallpaper, wall-to-wall carpet, tables covered with throws, and velvet upholstery create a cozy effect in the main room, above right. An eighteenth-century English clock and a Venetian painting called Agony in the Garden over the settee, opposite, are two of the few pieces in the apartment not Russian in origin.

■

Works by Gogol and Pushkin (from which Dostoevsky read to his children) mingle with ABC books and inkwells on the desk in the children's room, opposite. Bentwood chairs and a brass oil lamp, now electrified, are among the practical furnishings.

A corner of the study in which Dostoevsky died, above. His daughter recorded that his writing table was in perfect order at the time of his death, containing, in addition to a note from her, a Pushkin novel he'd been reading, a letter, and a receipt from a merchant.

DOSTOEVSKY

NEKRASOV

NIKOLAI ALEKSEEVICH NEKRASOV AND I.I. Panaev had an unusual number of things in common: an important literary journal of the mid-1800s, the woman they loved, and this apartment. Certainly, their living arrangement, whereby two generous sized apartments were joined together, facilitated their mutual infatuation with Panaev's wife. Progressive in all things, as co-publishers and co-editors they invited discussion and controversy, both at home and between the pages of their journal *Sovremennik* ("The Contemporary").

The apartment was the setting for crowded editorial meetings by day and animated social debate by night. Such topics as women's emancipation and reform of the political system figured in both. A spacious dining room and ballroom placed no restrictions on the size of guest lists. The literary critic and publicist P.A. Gaideburov commented, "These rooms heard so many arguments, so many thanks and reproaches, friendly greetings, and sharp threats. . . . The history of these rooms is the history of the literary relations of the whole epoch, the history of Russian journalism."

Nekrasov, whose rooms are shown here, was himself a writer. Some of his most important poetry and prose was produced in this apartment where he lived from 1857 to 1877. His success as an author, editor, and publisher shows in his home, a fine statement of bourgeois taste. The colors are sumptuous, the rooms rich with pattern, and the furniture well arranged both for receiving an unending flow of visitors and for aesthetic balance.

154

An 1884 painting by A. Naumov in the sitting room, below, *portrays Nekrasov and Panaev visiting their sick friend Belinsky. In the picture the three men cut short their political criticism as a servant announces the arrival of a policeman, seen through the doors.*

■

At the far end of the banquet room stands a small table for tea or intimate meals, opposite. *On it sits a portable samovar of Nekrasov's, which accompanied him on hunting expeditions, and a photo album, a customary conversation piece when visitors called.*

■

Overleaf: The writer's bedroom is shown as it was in the last year of his life. The divan is made up with linens, and a small table holds medicines and a brass bell. The setting was reconstructed from Nekrasov's death portrait, commissioned by him the year he died. The bust is of his friend Belinsky.

TCHAIKOVSKY

"I HAVE RENTED A HOUSE IN KLIN . . . large, comfortable, on the boulevard going to Moscow, it is outside the city . . . a peaceful, quiet corner, for work is always ready for me. . . . There is a splendid view from the window, and below a satisfactory garden. . . . What a blessing it is to know that no one will come, no one will interrupt neither work, reading, nor strolling!"

So wrote Pyotr Ilich Tchaikovsky of the great gray wooden house with white trim where he moved some few years before his death in 1893. Today the setting appears as warm and complete as when the composer still lived there. Upon Tchaikovsky's death, the house went to his brother Modest, who had the wisdom to convert it into a museum the following year.

The house was a sturdy shelter with plenty of space for study, composition, and music. But it was also a home, with an inviting library, comfortable living room, generous back porch, quiet sitting nook, and octagonal, enclosed sunporch—through all of which the composer and his dogs would amble. The rooms were decorated in a typical fashion of the nineteenth century. Seating groups of upholstered benches and chairs were organized around small tables, sharing the living room space with the piano. A sizable dining room that opened to the garden could host occasional guests with ease. A charming medley of jigsawed woodwork—employed universally in the late nineteenth century as ornament—gave great warmth to the library and adjacent hall. There is an appealing simplicity about the musician's bedroom, where rich color and pattern dressed a few conventional shapes in a stark almost modern way.

158

The composer's house is seen from the rear, right. *Its veranda leads to the garden from the dining room. A variety of patterns in trimwork punctuates the gray wood façade.*

■

In the living room, opposite top, portraits of composers and relatives surround the tile fireplace with its tapestry fire screen. The clock was made in Prague. An iron *bedstead, unadorned night stand, and embroidered slippers set the simple stage for sleep,* opposite bottom.

■

Page 160: *Decorative paneling creates an inviting sitting nook at the end of a corridor.* Page 161: *Jigsaw technique makes a warm woody envelope for the library. The large, hanging photograph is of Ilya Tchaikovsky, Pyotr's father.*

A small enclosed porch, above left, *furnished a tempting spot to muse or to take tea. The delicate embroideries draped over the dressing table, above right,* were a gift to the composer. The dining room, opposite, *opens onto the porch and garden.*

RUSSIAN HOUSES

CHEKHOV

ANTON PAVLOVICH CHEKHOV, ONE OF six children of a provincial shopkeeper, went to Moscow to study medicine and, to help support his studies, began to write humorous articles as a journalist. Until he moved to Yalta in 1889, Chekhov lived with his brother and sister in a modest home in Moscow. Each of the house's three small bedrooms was used by one of the Chekhovs, and Anton's doubled as an examination room for his patients. A common living room with a rich gold color scheme had a snug seating area facing a bank of windows that flooded the room with light.

Chekhov's house in the Crimea was more spacious, yet also homey. Having been ordered to move south for health reasons, he called it his "beautiful prison." At the age of thirty-nine the writer had contracted tuberculosis, which proved fatal only five years later. His *White Dacha* in Yalta was one of the most original, light-filled examples of residential architecture in the area. It was known for its modern, asymmetrical use of rugged coastal stone, its windowed tower and sunroom, and Arts-and-Crafts-style carved woodwork.

The doctor-turned-writer met and married an actress, Olga Knipper, after the Moscow Art Theater company stopped in Yalta to perform his *Seagull* and *Uncle Vanya*. Unfortunately, his wife was bound by her contractual agreement to return to act in Moscow while Chekhov's state of health required that he remain in his airy perch over the Black Sea. *The Cherry Orchard* and *Three Sisters* were written here. The *dacha* served as a kind of salon for such contemporaries as Maxim Gorky, Konstantin Stanislavsky, Feodor Chaliapin, and Sergei Rachmaninoff on their tours south.

164

A photograph of the writer in a turn-of-the-century frame, left. *He was characteristically pictured in frock coat, necktie, and spectacles. The then up-to-date interior details of the Yalta house*, opposite, *include a door with cutout woodwork and a small wall cabinet with painted carvings, both in the Arts and Crafts style.*

*I*n Yalta, the room of his wife, Olga Knipper-Chekhova, with her portrait, above. Cherry-red papered walls complement the nineteenth-century wooden furniture and crisply contrast with the traditional white linens on the brass bed.

∎

The design of the house, by L. N. Shapovalovyi,

was an original mix of vernacular architecture and turn-of-the-century themes with its off-center entry and tower, below.

∎

The writer was happy working in his garden, opposite: "If everyone would do everything on a piece of their own land, what a beautiful place our country would be."

∎

Page 168: The living room's pale colors and white slipcovers suit life by the sea. Page 169: Chekhov's study, where he wrote in the early mornings while others in the household slept, was described by a contemporary as "modest but airy." Stained glass was fashionable for the period.

∎

*T*he door to the pink stucco Moscow house where the Chekhovs lived, *right, is set back from the street in a small courtyard with a garden.*

■

Chekhov's sister's bedroom is delicately furnished with an iron bedstead, lacy linens, and flower-printed dresser throw, *above. Her sewing table sits in the clear light by a dormer window.*

■

A corner of the living room, opposite, shows more of the intensity of color of which Chekhov was apparently so fond.

The grouping of settee and chairs around a draped table is usual for a bourgeois house of the nineteenth century, as are the patterned wallpaper, oil lamp, and family photograph album bound in velvet.

■

ABRAMTSEVO

THE SIGNIFICANCE OF THE ART COLONY established in 1870 at Abramtsevo by Savva Ivanovich Mamontov lies not only in the architecture and design of its varied structures, but in the creative atmosphere it provided a group of celebrated artists. A stay there offered the chance to commune both with nature and with a dazzling array of luminaries from the fields of music, literature, and fine and applied arts, among them Mikhail Vrubel, Ilya Repin, Vasily Polenov, Viktor and Arkady Vasnetsov, and Valentin Serov. Feodor Chaliapin even serenaded the farmhands during haymaking.

This was a period in architecture and design that celebrated native culture and rejected slavish nineteenth-century styles. Industrial expressions were banished and natural themes embraced. Objects were created with a reverent understanding of materials, closely allying them with function.

The Arts and Crafts movement that William Morris inspired in England became a model for such ideals, as did the French art nouveau style. But Russians chose to return to their own roots and explored nature, folktales, crafts, religion, music, and traditional construction methods for new artistic direction. Their approach combined elements from the European schools filtered through the uniqueness of Russian culture.

The estate, which is about two hours from Moscow, had once belonged to the writer Sergei Aksakov. Mamontov set about building workshops for ceramics and woodcarving, a sculpture and painting studio, a guest house, and a private chapel on the grounds. All are of interest for the incorporation of medieval and folk motifs into their structures. While each differs distinctly from the others, each is representative of the time.

The large dining room of the main house hosted many dinners of Mamontov's family and celebrated friends, left. The fireplace was made of Abramtsevo tiles. Twelve-year-old Vera Mamontova was the subject of Girl with Peaches, *painted in this room by Valentin Serov in 1887. When the original painting was moved to a museum this copy was made.*

◾

The main house, built in eighteenth-century northern neoclassical style, opposite, was a model for the manor in Anton Chekhov's play The Cherry Orchard. *Its subdued color and subtle detail make it an unusually handsome example of a gentrified wooden mansion.*

Page 174: *Inside the guest cottage, Teremok, the furniture, icon case, and lidded boxes are fine examples of the carved woodwork made at the colony.* Page 175: *Tiles for the cottage's extraordinary fireplace were made outside the compound; the woodwork was carved at Abramtsevo.*

◾

The chapel, opposite top and above left, was the work of many artists who debated their plans at night around the tea table. Viktor Vasnetsov designed it in a combination of Novgorodian and Muscovite styles; Polenov planned the iconostasis; and both, in addition to Repin, Nevrev, and Vrubel contributed to the interior. Mamontov and his son are among those buried here.

∎

Alone or in company, guests could stroll along the lime tree allée, down shady paths, and over a series of bridges, opposite bottom, through birch groves, past the collection of charming Slavic Revival wooden buildings, and perhaps stop at the family chapel for a moment of quiet. The extraordinary lacework of the studio, above right, designed by V. A. Gartman in 1873, is a tribute to peasant craft.

∎

ABRAMTSEVO

VASNETSOV

THE HOUSE THAT PAINTER VIKTOR Mikhailovich Vasnetsov designed for himself is a colorful tribute to Russian folk culture. The artist is best known for his large-scale canvases depicting historical and folkloric characters and for his theater sets for productions with similar themes. His house is both personal and representative of the nostalgic period in which it was built.

Vasnetsov drew the plans for the house in 1893–1894 and had them executed by carpenters from Vladimir. The structure is a collage of motifs rooted in ancient timber architecture: interlocking log joints, cutout work used for exterior trim, exposed timber interior walls, and steeply pitched gables in the form of *bochki,* arches which shadow the domes of old wooden churches. He designed the interior as well, and most of the furniture was made by his brother, Arkady. The heavy, one-of-a-kind pieces are of oak and demonstrate the influence of the Arts and Crafts movement on the Slavic Revival style popular in Russia at the same time.

The artist, already known for the interior design of the Cathedral of Saint Vladimir in Kiev (a combination of Byzantine painting and mosaic), lived in this house for thirty productive years. He was an active member of the art colony at Abramtsevo, for which he designed the family chapel. In the studio here, among other important commissions, he completed the painting *Bogatyrs* which he had worked on for most of his creative life. Vasnetsov lived in this home with his wife and five children and died here at the age of seventy-eight.

178

The house's tower takes the form of a bochka, or church gable, left. Colorful roof tiles draw on a medieval motif. The two-story painting studio, opposite, was spacious enough for Vasnetsov's large-scale work. Paintings are (clockwise from top) Baba Yaga, the forest witch; Frog Queen—both from his folktale series; and Apocalypse, the study for a painting in the Saint Vladimir cathedral.

Page 180: *The main room,* top, *served for sitting and for entertaining guests. It contained a table, chairs, sofa, piano, and several cupboards. The Tower buffet,* bottom, *was made by the artist's brother. A portrait of Vasnetsov's daughter hangs nearby.* Page 181: *Seventeenth-century Roman chain mail and armor hang on a spiral staircase that led to the painting studio.*

■

VOLOSHIN

BY ALL ACCOUNTS, MAXIMILLIAN VOLO-
shin was well situated, living as he did in the town
of Koktebel in the Crimea. Not only did he reside
for most of his life in structures of his own design
(and, in part, his own construction), but he also
lived in an area traditionally linked to the legends
and mythic worlds of the Tatars and Greeks which
so interested him. Here the up-country mountains,
fragrant in spring with lush peonies, serve as backdrop to a rocky landscape that alternates sand
beaches with bays of carnelian pebbles. The entrance to the underworld is said to lie beneath one
of the region's boulders.

The writer moved here with his mother when he
was finishing his studies at gymnasium. She had
saved enough money to buy the land, and to
stretch their modest resources they set about
building their own house after the son's drawings.
He specified balconies on all sides to draw in the
brilliant light of the Black Sea. Voloshin's handi-
work shows in shelves, carved cupboards, daybeds,
and chairs. The interior has a very personal cast—
the marriage of undistinguished, commonly available furniture to Tatar textiles and collected and
homemade objects. Voloshin's fascination with
Egyptian and Greek culture shows in the mementos he brought back from his many trips to those
areas. There are treasures as well from his trips
to Italy, France, and Germany. His second wife,
Maria Stepanovna, saved a majority of the furnishings by burying them before the military occu-
pation of the area in 1941.

*Portraits of personal
heroes and friends
are grouped around bits
of Tatar textiles and a
shelf made by Voloshin,
left. Among the death
masks are those of Tol-
stoy, Pushkin, Gogol, and
Homer. A niche carved
out of the space on the
main floor beneath the
open studio/library, op-
posite, served as the spot
where Voloshin wrote.*

■

Overleaf: *Voloshin's
mother's room was
flooded with light and
appointed with a mix of
simple things, character-
istic of the house. A re-
gional weaving made a
Russian-style backdrop
for the bed. The divan
was layered in Tatar tex-
tiles and used bolsters as
armrests and backrests,
in harmony with the
Eastern weavings.*

■

POLENOV

EVEN BETTER THAN STYLISHLY RE-creating the ambience of a rustic life style in town by means of architecture and interior design was to actually forsake the city for the countryside. Vasily Polenov chose to live out the romantic provincial life, so idealized in the late nineteenth century, by moving to a bucolic site near the banks of the majestic Oka River. Known foremost as a landscape painter, Polenov left St. Petersburg to design his own home near a rural village. He dreamed of not only surrounding himself with nature, which was his chief inspiration, but also of establishing a small museum and arts center to benefit rural folk who had no access to urban temples of culture. For his students and friends who visited from town, his compound became, in the artist's words, a "nature academy."

Polenov accomplished his goals. He planned a house large enough to accommodate poetry evenings and even small theatrical shows, and also to sleep guests from the city. Its outward appearance is evocative of English Arts and Crafts architecture rather than of Russian timber style, the choice of many of Polenov's contemporaries. Nonetheless, Polenov incorporated enough woodwork and slavic-inspired furnishings into the house's interior to leave little doubt about his devotion to Mother Russia. He carefully planned the structure to afford glorious views of the river from the second-floor windows and from the garden terrace. He built a second, small building nearby which seemed to take its cue from French medieval monasteries. About it he wrote, "We have been living in the country where this summer I built a studio, but somehow it turned out as an abbey. Nonetheless, I am pleased...I dreamed about this my whole life, and now I can't believe it has been realized."

Around the library's table, left, *the family read, friends met to talk, and food was sometimes served. This space could be cleared for entertaining or for when plays were given by the village children.*

■

Among Polenov's collection of toys, opposite, *are figures said to be the original matryoshka dolls. The idea originated with Polenov's friend Malyutin, who made them as a gift.*

■

Page 188: *This paleontology collection is made up of pieces found near the river or while excavating for the house. The trompe l'oeil butterflies are by Polenov.* Page 189: *In the light-filled library, favorite works of Russian and European origin fill the spaces around the furniture and woodwork,* top. *Polenov's 1887 painting* Cemetery *hangs above an unusual cupboard-bench piece,* bottom.

■

REPIN

DETERMINED TO LEAVE THE BUSTLE OF St. Petersburg behind, painter and sculptor Ilya Efimovich Repin bought a tract of forested land near the Gulf of Finland. He designed a home for himself around a small single-story house that had been previously built there. On one side he added an enclosed veranda with a steeply pitched glass roof, which he used in warm weather for painting and sculpture. On another side an open veranda with a similar leaded-glass cap projected out toward the trees. He added a "winter" studio, heated by a large tile stove, on the second floor. Here and there, the sheet metal roof was raised with peaks and skylights, giving a beguiling, whimsical silhouette to the painted wood structure.

The interior is equally as unpredictable and uniquely attractive as the exterior. It is a place of narrow staircases, hidden doors, windows over windows, and jigsaw wooden trim work, all of which elaborate on motifs liberally adapted from

*izba*s (traditional wooden cabins) and churches. Generously scaled spaces provided the artist with plenty of work area. Throughout, the crystalline northern light penetrates to illuminate the rooms.

Penaty, the name Repin gave his estate after the Roman gods of the hearth, was frequented by the talented artists, writers, and academicians of the day: Ivan Pavlov, Maxim Gorky, Feodor Chaliapin, and others. On Wednesdays the artist and his wife, writer Natalya Nordman-Severova, hosted large dinner parties around a table of his design. The table was constructed with a center that turned like a lazy-Susan so that food could be reached by all, preempting the need for servants. According to the hosts' progressive *Rules of the Round Table*, "For breach of the principle of self-service a fine shall be due." The penalty was to deliver a witty speech from a raised rostrum across the room.

190

*P*enaty's hexagonal studio can be seen inside and outside, right and opposite. *The roofline of the house is an intriguing amalgam of volumes defined by windows and skylights that thoroughly illuminated the interiors for painting. Repin's bust of Tolstoy* stands on a pedestal, opposite. *Subjects sat for the artist atop the stairs.*

■

Page 192: *The winter studio, where a portrait of Pushkin remains unfinished, was large enough for many ongoing works,* top. *Many of Repin's paintings hang* in the dining room, bottom. Page 193: *The artist's last self-portrait sits on an easel by his palette. Later in life, when Repin began to suffer pain in his right hand, he rigged this palette to his waist and painted with his left.*

■

GORKY

IT IS IRONIC THAT MAXIM GORKY, A Marxist and early supporter of the Bolsheviks, ended his days in Moscow in such splendor. In May 1931, a few years before his death, he was given an art nouveau-style house. He decorated its large rooms with weighty furnishings of the period and fine Oriental art, including his collection of jade netsuke.

The house represents the best residential work of Fyodor Osipovich Shekhtel, an architect of international stature little known outside the Soviet Union, but whose work parallels that of Frank Lloyd Wright and Charles Rennie Mackintosh. A curvaceous limestone staircase is one of the house's outstanding elements. Its bronze lamp and backlit stained-glass panel were crafted in harmony with the architecture, as were all the original fittings in the house. A restoration of the site a few years ago brought out the polish of the brass hardware and handsomely carved woodwork, and the delicate colors of painted art nouveau motifs on walls and ceilings. The same cannot be said for the house's white brick façade with mosaics in naturalistic motifs, which remained in sore need of repair.

The house was originally commissioned in 1900 by the merchant Stepan P. Ryabushinsky, a great pre-Revolutionary patron of the arts and member of the Old Believers sect. Because the sect's religious practice was forbidden even before 1917 (its fundamentalist tenets were thought to stray too far from orthodoxy), Ryabushinsky had a secret chapel built up under the eaves of the house.

194

High-polish oak doors, right, were carved with different motifs for every room. The brass door handles are exceptionally delicate and understated.

■

The limestone staircase makes a fluid descent from the second to the main floor, opposite, and

defines the central hallway. Its curves are integrated even into the inlay work in the parquet floor. The stained-glass partition is thought to have been made in St. Petersburg. The lamp was designed by the architect.

■

*U*pstairs, a carved plaster capital crowns the staircase's decorative work, above left. Pale colors of paint contrast with deep wood tones throughout the spacious house.

■

Thematically unified architecture commands at- tention in the simply appointed entry, where the oak paneling is highlighted with brass, above right. The concentric rings of the floor pattern are marble and granite mosaic. Heavy draperies were closed as protection from drafts.

■

The comfortable living room has been refurnished in turn-of-the-century style, opposite. Architect Shekhtel made his own sketches for its ornamental ceiling. Skillful cabinetry shows in the valence and in the doors to this and other rooms.

■

BLOK

ALEXANDER ALEXANDROVICH BLOK happily returned to the unpretentious neighborhood of his childhood in 1912, and lived his last years there. He preferred this area on the outskirts of St. Petersburg to the westernized neoclassicism of the center city because he found it to be truly Russian. And he loved the quarter's quiet and simplicity. A private man, known for his expressions through verse, he preferred to keep to himself at home. His actress wife, Lyubov Dmitrievna, was more ebullient, however, and invited her own friends to visit often.

The lack of pomp in the rented apartment of the gifted symbolist poet is refreshing. The conventional railroad layout comprised Blok's study, a small dining room, two bedrooms, and a sitting room femininely decorated by Lyubov, where she received her visitors. A contemporary commented on the poet's study, "I look at the furniture: it is the most original I have ever seen. There is nothing superfluous in the room." Although the pieces were typical for the late nineteenth century, their spare arrangement represented something of a new approach. Books, essentials, and a collection of humorous animal memorabilia such as a charcoal drawing entitled *Pet Fish* nonetheless created an atmosphere with character and warmth.

198

The only piece of fine sculpture in the apartment is a bust of a woman by Mikhail Vrubel, which is placed on a simple stand by the poet's desk, left.

∎

In the dining room, opposite, two brass samovars stood by for tea.

One is of a lovely Jugendstil design, cleanlined, Germanic art nouveau. The teacups are assorted nineteenth-century pieces; those with the raised handles are typical of the Russian empire style. The enameled iron stove was moveable.

∎

200

*B*lok's bedroom, above, appointed with a cupboard, neo-Gothic folding screen, and small table and chair. His bed has been replaced by an upholstered bench. The jacket belonged to the poet; the photograph is of his wife.

■

The poet's study, opposite, was furnished simply, with a meeting table and sofa, as well as a desk and bookcases. A pat-terned table throw is rep-resentative of the period. Blok loved fresh flowers and always kept them at home. Both the pewter vase and the small can-dlestick on an end table show animal motifs.

CHALIAPIN

THE STYLE OF FEODOR IVANOVICH Chaliapin's apartment suited its expressive owner. Interesting combinations of rich texture and pattern created a background for antiques of various origins. It is a setting in which East meets West with delightful idiosyncrasy.

The opera singer moved to these premises in 1914, eight years before he made his permanent departure from the Soviet Union. He stayed a short time in America and then settled in Paris for the remaining sixteen years of his life. Chaliapin was as great a family man as he was an artist, and the convivial performer's apartment is filled with photographs and paintings of his children, relatives, and friends.

Not all the furnishings that remain in the flat are original, but those that are not have been chosen based on family recollections. Sharing a dominant position in the main living room are a grand piano and Chaliapin's life size favorite portrait of himself, by Boris Kustodiev. The painting shows him in a great fur coat and hat, out for a stroll with his dog, while the outdoor attractions of Russian winter provide a busy, theatrical backdrop. The dining room, a setting for many crowded gatherings, is furnished in weighty turn-of-the-century pieces. Its deep-colored walls are sparked by the jewel tones of an Oriental rug and a divan set up in Eastern fashion with a carpet throw and fringed pillows.

202

Bright highlights contrast with deep tones in the dining room, right and opposite top. The carved dining chairs, tablecloths, pillows, and carpets are originals. The paintings above the divan are by Konstantin Korovin. A collage of color and texture gives an Eastern feel to a portion of one sitting room, opposite bottom. The bowl is Venetian glass; the doll is from France.

A circa 1900 lamp and textured tile stove complement the moss greens of the dining room, opposite. All the furniture belonged to Chaliapin; a carved walnut chair near the stove was a gift from Gorky.

In the living room, above, framed photographs include one of Chekhov and Tolstoy.

■

Overleaf: The 1921 portrait of the singer was painted by Kustodiev. The photographs, paint-

ings, columns, and girandoles are original to the room. The furniture and piano are similar to those owned by Chaliapin. Above the ebony chest is a painting by Gausch.

■

CHALIAPIN

LENIN

LENIN SLEPT HERE. IN THE MODEST three-room flat of his friend and colleague Vladimir Bonch-Bruevich, the political leader sought shelter in the dangerous, pre-Revolutionary days of 1917. It was in this spartan room that he composed a most important document of that time, one of the linchpins of the Bolshevik philosophy: the decree which declared that land worked by the peasants should belong to them.

The head of the household, Bonch-Bruevich, resided in St. Petersburg, then called Petrograd, with his wife and daughter. As one of the most highly educated persons in the emerging communist party's hierarchy and director of its publishing arm, he acquired the rights to publish all of Lenin's, and also Maxim Gorky's, written works. Their manuscripts were kept in the apartment while he lived here. Bonch-Bruevich was made head of staff in Lenin's first government. An astute politician, he first sensed a weakening in the leader's power in 1920 and gracefully asked to retire because of health problems. He lived for another thirty-five years, serving the system in less controversial posts, first as director of the former serfs' agricultural organization and later as head of an antireligion museum.

An iron bedstead, washstand, and woodburning stove were among the few appointments in Lenin's room, left and opposite. A wooden bookcase across the room contained the small library he kept in the flat.

STANISLAVSKY

ONE OF THE GREAT NAMES IN RUSSIAN theater created a domestic set for himself that was deliberately spare. Konstantin Sergeevich Stanislavsky believed that "unnecessary things complicate life and interfere with one's work. One should only possess the most important articles for daily use and work." His is a refreshing philosophy— voiced as it was by one of the world's most gifted masters of artifice, the originator of the famous "method" of acting—rare in Russian home design, and reflecting a modern, twentieth-century point of view.

Stanislavsky was a name that he had adopted to spare his family the embarrassment of his taking up a trade still considered improper. He then went on to devote his life to making acting an honorable profession.

Stanislavsky moved into this apartment in 1921, after he was made director of the Opera Studio of the Bolshoi Theater. Three years later, the studio broke its affiliation with the Bolshoi and afterwards became known as the Stanislavsky Opera-Theater Studio. Actors, set painters, and opera singers studied with him, as he put it, "to improve vocal culture...and stage culture."

The day began in the blue foyer, where his pupils signed in and later would return to relax during breaks. The space also served as an anteroom for an adjacent ballroom where performances were staged. Real work got underway in the study, set up informally like a living room, but with large bookcases that were positioned so as to create wings from which actors could make their entrances. The master presided from a sofa, with his papers on a small table. For years he slept and wrote in the study too, giving credence to his home-as-workshop approach.

The dramatic blue of the foyer set the tone of the work day, right. *The columns are faux marbre. Stanislavsky bought the marble table from the flat's previous owners; arriving students signed a book kept here.*

The dining room furniture, opposite, *had been moved from Stanislavsky's former apartment. It was sometimes shrouded with white slipcovers, in the style of many Russian homes, adding an appealingly wrinkled freshness. Portraits of his great-grandparents flank a nineteenth-century cupboard. Upholstered chairs were tapestry covered.*

∎

PASTERNAK

AT THE END OF A LANE OF LEAFY birches stands a quiet, brown wooden house. On a sunny October afternoon forty years ago, Boris Leonidovich Pasternak would have been outside pruning fruit trees or sitting around a table in the garden with friends, the samovar bubbling to refresh glasses of tea. The poet and novelist, whose masterpiece *Doctor Zhivago* has only recently been published for the first time in his native country, is buried nearby in the village cemetery.

Until a short time ago, his *dacha* was empty, the Nobel laureate's furniture having been removed by force within the last decade, a time when his work was still in disfavor. The house had been used in season by his descendants until then. The gabled, turn-of-the-century style *dacha* is one of many in the writers' colony outside Moscow called Peredelkino, a forested area that cloisters private country homes of the members of the officially sanctioned Writers' Union.

Although the house was built in 1937 as a summer place, once *Doctor Zhivago* was published abroad but publicly condemned at home, Pasternak increasingly spent time there year-round, absorbed in the pleasures of gardening. Pasternak wrote the book both at his *dacha* and in his Moscow flat. Today only two rooms in the flat remain as they were in the author's time. One is his study, with its stand-up writing desk and leather-covered worktable, where the family would gather to hear Pasternak read chapters of *Doctor Zhivago* before the book was finished. The other is his bedroom, where a portion of the original *Zhivago* manuscript lies tied in marbled paper.

212

A solitary rattan chaise stands on the dacha's *side porch, right. The house had been only nominally maintained until recently, when the writer's reputation was officially restored. Pasternak's elegant, simple grave in the village nearby is continuously bedecked with offerings,* opposite. *Russians typically honor their great literary heroes in such a manner.*

■

Page 214: *Among the personal effects remaining in his bedroom in Moscow is a framed photograph of Jawaharlal Nehru inscribed, "With warm regards to Boris Pasternak", sent as congratulations in 1958, when Pasternak was awarded the Nobel Prize.* Page 215: *Solemn and simple is the tone set by his study. In later years, problems with his legs obliged Pasternak to work standing up.*

■

CONTEMPORARY LIFE

CONTEMPORARY LIFE

AFTER THE REVOLUTION, RUSSIAN cities were inundated with people seeking opportunity and fleeing the growing famine in the countryside. Workers considered themselves lucky to be apportioned even a bunk or a corner of a room in makeshift barracks and dormitories. Caught off guard by the flood of new arrivals, the Bolshevik government struggled to find accommodations for them. In the early 1920s, the utopian idea of the garden city took hold, and compact houses were built for the workers on small plots of land, drawing on the appeal of the *dacha*. But this sort of housing soon proved too costly. The government began to build massive projects and it nationalized numerous private homes. Where previously one family had enjoyed ten rooms, now ten families shared a common kitchen and bathroom. Many of these communal apartments still exist today.

Multifamily apartments had little to recommend them. With kitchen and bath facilities shared by many, conditions were often squalid. Each family had its own separately metered gas burner, but to avoid theft the inhabitants had to carry their pots, pans, and food back and forth between kitchen and living room for every meal. As for the bathroom, tenants devised complicated systems of queues, and tempers understandly ran high. Yet, despite the feuding and the crowding, these accom-modations were a source of envy to those unable to find any place at all.

In his 1925 story "The Crisis," Mikhail Zoshchenko satirized the housing problems of early Soviet life. Zoshchenko's hero scours Moscow in search of a room, unable to find even a place to shave. Finally, unkempt and unbathed after two weeks, he learns that for thirty rubles a month he can be fixed up in a bathroom, equipped with not only a door for privacy, but a marble tub with brass fittings. The hero manages to find himself a wife, and within a year the couple has a child. Their domestic life would be blissful if only the other thirty-one tenants of the apartment did not demand a daily bath, displacing the family each evening. When the hero's mother-in-law arrives from the village and moves in behind the hot-water tank, he loses patience and flees his coveted living space, also deserting his wife and child.

While Zoshchenko's story is humorous, the reality behind it is sobering. The paucity of housing, initially an inconvenience, soon resulted in real misery. The overcrowding led to increased alcoholism, crime, and divorce, and the social restiveness of a large portion of the population became a political liability, one that has persisted to the present time. Every Soviet leader has attempted to meet the need for new housing by initiating ambitious programs of construction, transforming city

skylines with ugly, if functional, apartment complexes.

At various times a concern for aesthetics has manifested itself, as at the end of the 1920s, Moscow town planners enlisted the aid of some remarkable artists and architects to create visual harmony in the city by color-coordinating individual streets. The project, however, was never realized. Throughout the early Soviet period, visionary architects planned radical dwellings that contrasted strongly with the utilitarian behemoths the state was constructing. Such architects as El Lissitzky dreamed of changing through design the way people lived and thought. Lissitzky demanded an "architecture for world revolution," calling for living spaces that would stimulate the modern consciousness and help humanity realize its full potential. Kazimir Malevich focused his attention on the cosmos in his design for geometric *planity,* free-floating dwellings in space. The *planity* were part of larger "aerocities" linked to settlements on earth. Malevich's idea was that life in space could free people both physically and emotionally from their earthly limitations.

One of the Soviet Union's most brilliant architects was Konstantin Melnikov, who built his own house in Moscow in 1927—striking for its cylindrical form and more than sixty hexagonal windows. Despite its modern design, the house relies on such Russian traditions as plaster-covered brick, derived from church architecture, and built-in furniture, from peasant construction. In place of beds, Melnikov used stone pedestals, some of which he positioned behind screens, following the nineteenth-century bourgeois custom. Melnikov hoped that his design would point the way to a new style of building, but to his disappointment the house was interpreted as a personal statement entirely inappropriate to the needs of a communal society.

Most people could not even dream of building their own house. Desperate for work, they had given up their rural cottages for a few square feet of space in the city. Their urban dwellings, once secured, offered electricity and indoor plumbing, but such luxuries could not make up for the comfort and warmth of masonry and wood lost in the transition to concrete and steel.

Once Stalin consolidated his rule in 1928, he wielded his power even in the sphere of public housing, commissioning grandiose buildings to mark the glory of his reign. Many of these buildings were too overblown to be graceful, giving rise to the moniker "Stalinist Gothic." Still, they were remarkably well built, even if the quality of construction reflected fear of Stalin's disapproval more than workers' pride. The architects of the period inventively reinterpreted eighteenth-century classicism for Soviet society, embellishing buildings with caryatids of industrious workers in place of the traditional mythological figures. Inside, the apartments were light-filled and spacious, with large windows and high ceilings. Today these dwellings are highly prized, especially in comparison to those built under successive leaders.

The later apartments were constructed much more rapidly, with little consideration either for materials or workmanship, a fact made apparent by their crumbling exteriors. Under Khrushchev in the 1960s, there sprang up a whole series of *khrush-choby,* a word coined by combining the leader's name with the Russian word for slum, *trushchoby.* These five-story rectangular apartment blocks lacked any sense of taste or individuality. Worse yet were the myriad "microregions" of Brezhnev's rule, which disfigured the outskirts of Soviet cities with miles of identical concrete high-rises. Drab and impersonal, appearing eternally to be under construction, these buildings impress upon their residents a monotony that is difficult to escape. Yet the apartments in these microregions are much sought after for the simple reason that they are designed for single-family use. Romantic as it may appear to live in a former palace amid ornate woodwork and elegant friezes, most of the old apartments in the city centers are still communal and in poor repair.

Current Soviet law allows for only thirty square feet of living space per person, and waiting lists for housing are so long that parents regularly sign up their infants in the hope that the children will receive a place of their own by the time they are in their twenties. Three generations commonly share the same apartment, and convenient as this may be for child care, it is not easy in day-to-day life. Many are savvy enough to find ways to live in less cramped quarters, however. In his 1976 true-to-life novel *The Ivankiad,* Vladimir Voinovich details the wily and desperate maneuverings of a Muscovite writer trying to get a two-room apartment for himself and his pregnant wife. The bureaucratic snares he encounters seem truly fantastic to anyone unschooled in the workings of the Soviet system. But Russians are nothing if not resourceful, and they have learned to cope with their housing difficulties. Unofficial apartment exchanges continually take place as the number of necessary rooms increases or decreases depending on changing family situations, adding further complications to divorce and remarriage.

The sleeping arrangements in present-day apartments may reflect tradition as much as the cramped conditions of Soviet life. Western visitors always wonder where all the family members sleep. If five people live in two rooms plus a kitchen, there just does not seem to be enough space. But eventually it becomes clear that the living/dining room where the visitor feasts is actually a bedroom, while the couch in the second room turns into a bed at night. And in the end such arrangements are not so different from the haphazard sleeping accommodations of nineteenth-century bourgeois homes, though Soviet citizens will insist they live that way because of the housing crisis, which has persisted at least since 1917.

Russians avoid feeling claustrophobic by spending a great deal of time outdoors. In the Soviet era, the public park has replaced the private home as a place for relaxation, and even the grimmest microregions have a nearby birch or pine forest. Better yet is the countryside, to which urban Russians flock whenever they have a chance. Most families have a country place,

222

or *dacha,* even if it is only a rented room. The idea of a simple life close to nature remains strong. Though the *dacha* offers greater informality and often more living space, its real appeal lies in the surrounding woods, bursting with mushrooms and berries, which are avidly picked in yearly rituals. During the summer Russians spend as many days as possible in the country; in the winter they make weekend forays for cross-country skiing.

Most of the year must be spent at home, however, and the Russians have managed to make their modest apartments quite attractive, despite a staggering scarcity of materials. Even a simple remodeling project demands heroic efforts to search out materials and cajole delivery. The ability to make something out of nothing reflects the Russian respect for self-sufficiency, ingenuity, and beauty. Entering a private apartment can be like entering another world, particularly after encountering the undifferentiated exteriors and public areas of most residential buildings. Such tiny apartments often impart an impression of excessiveness and European eccentricity, stuffed chockablock as they are with artwork and collectibles. Whether the objects are expensive antiques or handmade crafts, they define the owners' individuality and reveal a particularly Russian taste for ornamentation and eclecticism. Frequenting secondhand stores has become a great pastime, even an obsession, for many Russians. There they can buy pre-Revolutionary paintings and furniture betokening an idealized past. People spend seemingly exorbitant sums for offbeat items, but then, rents average only 4 percent of a worker's monthly salary.

Shopping for items to decorate the home takes on additional meaning in Soviet society, where all of one's skills must be used to seek out available items. Often the most interesting or valuable objects do not appear on the shelves but are squirreled away by prior agreement through a complicated system of bribes and back-scratching. Taking part in this wheeling and dealing allows the Soviet citizen to exert a certain independence and thus represents not only bohemianism, but also a mild form of rebellion in a tightly controlled society. Much of the impassioned activity in Soviet life takes place on the sly.

Despite the demands of practicality in the Soviet era, the ideal of home remains unchanged. It must offer a haven from the elements, whether natural or political. Home is also a bright spot, a cozy hearth now heated by oil burners instead of masonry stoves, but with no less spirit. The Russians know that a comfortable home can bolster its inhabitants. It can also reflect their characters. An old proverb says, "As your home is, so are you." Modern-day Russians have taken this adage to heart, struggling against all odds to create habitats that reflect their warmth, humor, resilience, and vitality.

BRUSSILOWSKY

TWENTY YEARS AGO, WHEN ANATOLY Brussilowsky began to furnish his Moscow apartment, most who could afford such luxuries longed for imperial period antiques or wanted to trade up to new furniture from Eastern Europe. That suited the underground painter just fine, as he was one of the few who cared for what official critics dubbed babushka's style: turn-of-the-century furniture and glass, which others were forsaking.

Brussilowsky longed to re-create the warm ambience of his childhood in Odessa and the atmosphere of his grandparents' spacious home, decorated in art nouveau style. All of it had been lost after the Bolsheviks took power, and eventually his relatives had been evacuated to Siberia. With his memories as a guide, Brussilowsky began to discover desired objects in private hands, and offered to trade new furniture or other sought after goods for them. As families fell from grace, they sometimes had to unload their possessions quickly, and trading for money or even food was welcome. Brussilowsky also found collectibles in the scrap heaps: the discards of party faithfuls who considered late-nineteenth-century trappings to be tarnished reminders of an unenlightened past or of people moving to more modest flats. Later, as his art brought him success, he acquired pieces through his network of collectors—presently the most common method used by Soviets to accumulate antiques.

The studio area of Brussilowsky's apartment is chockablock full of his extraordinary finds. His erotic and political art can now be shown openly. His collages, canvases, and seriagraphs mix unself-consciously with suites of rare Russian art nouveau furniture, French Daum glass, and tokens of his childhood. Providing a colorful, contextual backdrop are wall-to-wall native area rugs and shawls hung for a tented effect.

A suite of Russian art nouveau chairs and settee with silk velvet upholstery, thought to be by Meltzer, right, is squeezed around a table draped with a length of Syrian velvet. Zodiac-

inspired silkscreens line the walls behind. Brussilowsky's Perestroika series in collage with airbrush is shown on his desk amid turn-of-the-century lamps and brass decorative objects, opposite.

*R*ussian love of color and pattern is taken to the limit, above. *An overall look at the atelier reveals little of its physical shell. Shawls tacked all across the slanted ceiling and wall-to-wall rugs create a bright textile envelope for the owner's art nouveau treasures. The rugs are Ukrainian and Moldavian kilims.*

Near the entry stand a Venetian blackamoor, a late-nineteenth-century Russian gilded chair with a wild boar throw, and Brussilowsky's stuffed lion from childhood, opposite. The tapestry hanging behind is the artist's own creation.

■

Overleaf: *Part of the owner's extensive collec-*

tion of French art nouveau glass is grouped on a sideboard for impact. The pieces are lit from within by jury-rigging bulbs and wires through them to bring their patterns to life. The lamp is Lalique, and most of the vases are Galle.

■

Page 230: *Cherubs emerge in deep relief on a*

tall bronze vase. Neither the vase nor the small silver bowls show any creator's markings. Frequently in Russia flowers are dried to use decoratively since fresh ones are so dear. Page 231: A collection of Russian eggs are displayed on a tray with Kuznitzov porcelain vegetables behind.

■

MELNIKOV

THE REMARKABLE HOUSE ARCHITECT Konstantin Melnikov built for his family in 1927 stands apart in the Soviet Union today, a landmark of international significance, and one of the few extant single-family houses in Moscow. The burden of maintaining the unique structure is the price paid by Melnikov's son and daughter for their continued habitation of their home.

In 1925 Melnikov won the gold medal at the Paris World's Fair for what Josef Hoffmann, the director of the prestigious Wiener Werkstätte, hailed as "the best pavilion of the entire exhibition." On his return to Moscow, a high party official put land at Melnikov's disposal for his own dwelling. Unlikely as it seems, for a period of time the construction of single-family dwellings was an accepted means of increasing the severely impoverished housing stock, so Melnikov was not alone in gaining permission for such a project. But the fact that he emblazoned his signature across the front of the house in stucco relief was later seen as a showy bourgeois gesture.

Interestingly, Melnikov's house predates the breakthrough work of most of his more celebrated contemporaries, such as Mies van der Rohe, Le Corbusier, and Gerrit Rietveld. Further, its interlocking cylinder plan immediately set it apart from the others' work. The architect devised a system for self-reinforcing floors, by means of a wafflelike grid, thereby eliminating the need for internal bearing walls. Some of the furniture was built-in in such a fashion as to underline the value he put on light, fresh air, and cleanliness—thoroughly modern ideals. At the same time he looked to historical models as diverse as classical architecture and seventeenth-century Russian fortifications for inspiration in his work.

232

*T*he northern exposure of the vertical house has a honeycomb look, achieved with hexagonal windows, a form adapted from pierced ramparts, left. Utilities, bedrooms, and studio are stacked in this three-story cylinder. To form the façade, one wall of the two-story southern cylinder is flattened with a window wall. A roof terrace tops this section, with access from the third-floor studio.

■

Melnikov's studio, where he instructed architecture students, opposite, was flooded with northern light. Today his son, Victor, uses the space as his painting studio.

■

*T*he intersection of the cylinders creates space for a staircase that spirals through the core of the house, an area highlighted by green paint. The living room is now used as a library, above. Portraits of the architect's parents, who were peasants, hang adjacent to a tile stove with a constructivist form, above right.

In the third-floor studio, opposite, a wash of yellow marks the outside of the stairwell and is picked up in the railing of the perch Melnikov fashioned for himself. Here he could work by himself and survey his students' progress. French doors lead from Melnikov's work platform to the terrace atop the house's southern cylinder.

RUSSIAN HOUSES

*I*n a revolutionary design for optimum ventilation and light, the sleeping areas for the family of four opened onto each other, with only slim partitions separating them into three wedge-shaped segments, opposite and above.

∎

A painting, opposite bottom, *shows the original arrangement of masonry platform beds. Conventional nineteenth-century furniture has replaced the original built-in pieces, and the entire space has become a bedroom and sitting room for Melnikov's daughter.*

MELNIKOV

JUNGER

ACTRESS HELENA JUNGER HAS MAN-aged to retain by herself the apartment she used to share with her husband, the well-known theater director Nikolai Akimov, and their daughter. The couple met when she was auditioning for a company he was organizing in the early 1930s. She went on to play Viola in his production of Shakespeare's *Twelfth Night* and she continues to act today. Akimov was a much-praised director whose repertoire included classic English and French and contemporary Russian works. Denounced during the Stalin years, he eventually lost his post, but he continued to create the stylized portraits in pastel, watercolor, and gouache that give character to the walls of his rooms.

In memory of her husband, the actress keeps his office and studio as they were when he died in 1968. Rather than disturb the articles that link her to their shared life in the theater, Mrs. Junger has created a bedroom/sitting room for herself elsewhere in the apartment, where she can also take her meals. Like many Soviet citizens self-schooled in the acceptance of physical limits, she is particularly adept at carving many uses out of the one space in which she spends most of her time.

Far from feeling like musty museum rooms, the sky-blue office and adjoining studio are flooded with daylight, thanks to the French doors which open onto a southern exposure near a river embankment in the heart of Leningrad. And Akimov's well-cared-for personal furnishings and on-the-mark portraits of his students keep a certain youthfulness in the rooms.

*A*kimov's portraits of *friends and family are seen,* below. *In a corner of his studio, opposite, are a pair of French nautical scenes, a set of* figures based on Twelfth Night, *handmade by a fan who attended every performance, a door decorated with upholstery tacks, and church ornaments.*

■

Page 240: *The seating area in the room Helena Junger puts to everyday use,* top, *has modern Russian furniture and a lamp she created using a centuries-old iron taper stand, topped with a Korean straw hat and decorated with fans and natural trinkets from her* travels. *Her husband's paintings, family photographs, and other art crowd the walls. Seen through the doorway, "Peter the Great's corner" of the study,* bottom, *is so called for the central table of the period.*

■

Page 241: *Amid Russian empire-style furniture in the study stands a twentieth-century dog figure which survived the nine-hundred-day siege of Leningrad intact while its owners had to abandon their home.*

MOROZOVA

THE STYLES OF MOST CONTEMPORARY Russian homes evolve from a particular interest or reflect materials available to certain people at a specific time. Lara Morozova's home, however, could be said to be decorated in the Western sense of the word. The atmosphere and arrangement of objects have surely been influenced by its owner's trips abroad and her knowledge of antiques.

Mrs. Morozova was fortunate to have inherited some interesting furnishings. Cultivated taste has helped her take advantage of professional connections and family ties, not only to build several worthwhile collections, but to create a refined atmosphere in which to display the beautiful objects. Her Moscow apartment, more spacious than most, affords her the framework to showcase her possessions, including the porcelain, beadwork, lacquered boxes, and icons in which she takes a special interest. Each of the four rooms is wallpapered and carpeted, and her fine antique furniture, most from the nineteenth century, is put to everyday use. The Russian proclivity for pattern shows here, but the prints are subtle and the color subdued.

In the living room, family portraits and antique miniatures are grouped to define the seating area. Console tables are symmetrically appointed with eighteenth- and nineteenth-century accessories. The dining room stands open to the living room on one side and the kitchen on another, an uncommon arrangement. The kitchen is also deliberately designed, for which Mrs. Morozova had a castoff nineteenth-century cupboard reworked and pieced together for cabinets. Even a microwave oven finds a spot here. In the bedroom a wall of icons twinkles across from the bed, with its hundred-year-old crocheted coverlet. The owner pays no mind as her dog bounds up on it: "I don't worry. Things survive people."

242

Above a nineteenth-century sofa, a collection of miniatures is arranged, some of which are likenesses of relatives or ancestors' family friends, right. *The silhouettes in ivory and eglomise are rare. Mrs. Morozova's own portrait, rendered in a traditional style by the artist Shilov, hangs above. The sconces are in early-nineteenth-century style.*

On the bedroom wall, opposite top, *hang icons from the sixteenth to eighteenth centuries. Most of the furniture is Russian, made in the nineteenth century. An eighteenth-century lamp, now electrified, sits on the tabletop next to a small travel bar made of poplar. The bedspread is a crochet-on-linen piece from the nineteenth century.*

■

A Russian mahogany console is one of a pair which, when joined together with leaves, forms a table for forty, opposite bottom. *On it, an eighteenth-century English Norton clock, an opal glass vase, nineteenth-century Russian candelabra with crystal and ruby glass bases, and a precious commodity these days— fresh long-stemmed roses.*

A collection of porce-
lain cups and sau-
cers fills a mahogany
cabinet in the dining
room, opposite. *Most of
them are Russian: some
early-nineteenth-century
pieces from the Gardner
factory, some re-editions
of imperial porcelain.*

■

In the kitchen, above left,
samovars and trays fill
niches in cabinets fash-
ioned from a nineteenth-
century cupboard. *Such
custom cabinetry and
modern appliances make
this an exceptional kitch-
en installation. Mrs.
Morozova collects
nineteenth-century bead-
work and lacquered boxes
from the village of Palekh,*
above right.

■

JUTOVSKI

IN THE UNOFFICIAL SOVIET ART world, having a separate space as a painting studio is a sign of achievement. Boris Jutovski did not come by his easily. Like many others now heralded as contemporary cultural heroes, he remained true to his ideals, working in the underground art community for many years. Although these artists' work was not officially approved, they did gain a measure of recognition among their own ranks and through sales to the West.

By 1962 Jutovski had made something of a name for himself when he was invited to participate in a ground-breaking show in Moscow. It was an exhibition that gave the first public exposure to many young artists, as well as to formerly unshown masters of the 1920s. This pause in post-Revolutionary political history was an unpredictable moment of relaxation, when Khrushchev created the climate for a loosening of restraint, and then was vociferously horrified by the results.

One of the canvases from that show is given a prominent place in Jutovski's studio. It is one of the paintings that Khrushchev had singled out as an example of the worthlessness of modern art. Later, in the kind of turnaround so common to Soviet life, the vituperative head of state and the artist made up and became friends.

In the past thirty years, Jutovski has developed a wide range of work that can be characterized as colorful and expressive. His studio shares the same qualities. Although simply furnished, the three rooms can provide for all his needs when he makes camp there for a period of concentrated work. While his valuables are kept elsewhere, here he's given attention to the arrangement of meaningful souvenirs and favored bric-a-brac.

*J*utovski's portrait *which Khrushchev decried hangs near a candid photo of the leader and a posed color photograph of artist friends in an antique frame, left. An assemblage of unique* pieces, right, *form an unfinished work which the artist began to mark his fiftieth year. Opposite, the kitchen table, with gaily painted teacups from Uzbekistan drying on a tea towel.*

GORELIK

THEIR FAMILY OF FOUR FITS SNUGLY into the three rooms plus kitchen allotted Angelina and Alex Gorelik. Limited floor space does little to dampen the spirits of these lovers of literature and avid collectors. Their books, some of them rare, overflow the floor-to-ceiling shelves that climb nearly all the walls. But logic pervades. Manuscripts can be plucked down for perusal at a moment's notice. Even the stacks on the floor are orderly. An object can be readily unearthed from burgeoning shelves to elicit from the owners a knowing descripton of its origins.

An upright piano finds a place in the main room amid volumes and collected bits of art. The study, equally as book-laden but distinguished from the other room by virtue of its desk, is used mainly by Alex, an engineer. Daybeds propped with pillows help convert both rooms into sleeping areas at night. Though the kitchen is cramped, with a small table and as many chairs or stools as will fit around it when friends come to share a meal, space is always made for one more. The Goreliks' two young daughters have the only bedroom to themselves, so they can retreat when dinners evolve into late-night discussions.

Like other Russians with a good eye and a taste for mementos of their country's past, the Goreliks have found some odd pieces as castoffs. Some of their possessions are valuable and they have traded with collectors or purchased items that hold special interest. And some they have made, such as the lamp that hangs over the main room's game table. It symbolizes three of their favorite pastimes: cards, chess, and dice. Alex laughs, "Of course we like drinking too, but we couldn't think of a way to get it into the lamp."

A 1970 painting by naive artist Gennady Pavlov, right, depicts apartment houses in the back streets of Moscow while commenting on the dwarfing impact of Soviet urban life.

∎

The view from the study, opposite, shows that bookshelves climb the hallway's walls too. Treasures are wedged in among the volumes in the study. On the door hangs a 1922 map of Moscow bordered by commercial slogans, unusual because it was made at a time when Lenin permitted cooperatives to advertise.

∎

Page 250: Alex Gorelik works at a desk surrounded by things he loves. They include a white marble Mongolian idol, a cast-off half-torso in ebony, and a nineteenth-century barometer with Cyrillic characters.

∎

Page 251: The main room features a piano, game tables, and a homemade lamp. The two chess sets were made by prisoners in camps: one seventeen years ago, by a peasant in Siberia, and one by a German prisoner of war in 1945. Nearby, in a stack of manuscripts, is a rare diary kept by Tolstoy's secretary when the author left his home just before his death.

KAPELUSH

EMIL KAPELUSH HAS BEEN A SET DE-signer for over a dozen years and his vocational ingenuity is equally challenged at home by creating "life sets" in the tiny rooms of the family's fifth-floor walk-up in Leningrad. As is common with Russian parents, Emil and his wife, Irina, have chosen to allot one entire room to their daughter so that she can have free rein for study, play, and painting. Another room is set up for work, sitting, and the adults' sleeping accommodations. The kitchen also serves as the entry to the apartment, and an arrangement of table and chairs in the alcove beyond creates additional room for dining, reading, or painting.

For Emil, the tabletops and shelves form lilliputian stages where he makes further imaginative use of his skills in playing with shape, proportion, and space. Still lifes may be composed of laboratory glass, wood turnings, and shells, combined with papier-mâché figures he has made or with his miniature folkloric paintings. In addition, Emil has been executing canvases of a more serious nature for about seven years, some of which are kept at home while others are exhibited in the city's smaller museum shows, or have been purchased by foreigners.

His touch is noticeable throughout the apartment, where curtains have been sewn from left-over theater fabric, bits of mirror and glass bounce light into darker corners, and a painted triptych is made of wood scraps and moldings.

252

D raped fabric play-fully provides a backdrop for kitchen things in the space over the refrigerator, left. On another wall, personal hygiene and food preparation vie for space, opposite. Condiment boxes hung on the wall are painted with Emil's appealing miniatures.

■

Overleaf: A side table covered with velvet becomes a small stage for a grouping of papier-mâché figures with extraordinary detailing made by the owner. He uses painted wood turnings, bell jars, and shells to create environments for the figures.

SANOVICH

RETIRED ORIENTALIST IGOR SANOVICH had the foresight to acquire artwork from the underground community of artists when such works had no approved worth, and from collectors who encountered hard times and were forced to sell their possessions. Now his burgeoning flat, in one of the monolithic apartment buildings that ring the city, looks more like an attic than a home.

He sits at a desk all but overrun by treasures and personal mementos. Across the room a small television peeks out of a bookcase laden with statuary and books. Igor explains this rather extraordinary setting: "When I started collecting forty years ago, the museums were closed. The government didn't consider them important. Nothing was being bought. Sometimes I traded for things. There were still antique stores then, and curio shops. And I bought from painters before they became famous. In the fifties you could even buy Malevich, Chagall, the avant-gardists." Now, his and other discerning collectors' assets have been augmented by the approbation of the international art world and the heightened value of material goods in a deeply troubled economy.

Igor is a stunning example of the passionate contemporary Soviet collector who gladly sacrifices living space to remembrances of their country's cultural past. Some years ago eighty of his icons were stolen, reportedly in a KGB raid. Nevertheless his inventory still runs the gamut from thirteenth-century religious artifacts through twentieth-century folk art, incorporating both his serious taste in art and his wry sense of humor. Today such a collection would be all but impossible to amass.

Twentieth-century wooden toys share space with eighteenth-century religious sculpture, chunks of semiprecious stones, and a Chinese cloisonné bird, right. Behind them, a Peter the Great–style coffer banded in iron and a French boule box.

■

A Russian secretary, made in 1723, dominates a corner filled with figurines, vases, and contemporary art, opposite. The desk of pine, maple, and poplar veneer was found in a rubbish heap, where it was likely tossed by someone moving to smaller quarters. The erector-set dog was made by the young painter Nikita Gashunin, before his art brought him success.

■

Page 258: Two works by Georgian naive painter Pirosmani, Camel with a Guide and Two Georgians with a Jug of Wine, hang above a grouping of religious sculpture, diminutive Persian figures, and sundry pieces. Page 259: In another corner, a Persian painting from the eighteenth century faces a portrait of a Russian freemason from the same era, amid folk dolls and fragments of church ornament.

■

260

*I*n the full-to-brimming kitchen, above, *Russian, Persian, and central Asian pottery fill spaces around appliances.*

∎

As in many contemporary apartments, beds bedecked with Persian carpets provide seating area during the day. Such a daybed, *opposite, backs up to the owner's desk, a work surface virtually covered with personal mementos, books, and figurines. Icons adorn the walls. A Christ figure from the sixteenth-*century hangs to the left of shelves which house porcelain treasures.

∎

Overleaf: *An eighteenth-century Italian peacock chair adds unusual texture to the layers of paintings and Oriental figures. The black table* with mother-of-pearl inlay is thought to be from nineteenth-century Europe. On top of it stands an Italian baroque jasper cabinet inlaid with various types of the stone, made in the mid-seventeenth century.

∎

SCIENTIST'S DACHA

HIGH VALUE HAS ALWAYS BEEN placed on having a country house, or *dacha*. Not only do city dwellers living in extremely cramped conditions long for more space, but Russians have traditionally been great nature lovers. Compounds of *dachas* are reserved by profession for highly placed individuals. Thus, well-regarded members of the Writers' Union are ensconced in one such enclave in the woods at Peredelkino, privileged scientists are lodged in another area, and so forth.

This house, originally built of logs in about 1930, was expanded in 1946 and given to a scientist and educator for year-round living. When he was ousted, the *dacha* was confiscated and divided. The main floor was awarded to another member of the scientific community for weekend and holiday use, while the top floor was given to a separate family.

In the downstairs portion, the large sunroom acts as the main living space in season. There people can stretch out with a good book, dine, or take tea. Barefoot grandchildren weave through a group of adults engaged in more or less serious conversation. Toys lie where they are discarded. Sounds of someone sawing wood float in through open windows. There is no hurry to clear the table after the meal, someone else may still show up. In short, the atmosphere is relaxed.

The room itself is modeled in spirit on *Penaty*, the estate of nineteenth-century painter Ilya Repin, where a large round table was also placed at the core of the space. This table at the *dacha*, which seats twelve with ease, is a copy of one designed by Repin. It functions well for a crowd because of its built-in central turntable, a lazy Susan of sorts where serving dishes are rotated, and nothing is out of reach.

The rear of the dacha faces the woods, right. Decorative white railings are reminiscent of the pierced trim work of centuries-old timber houses, or izbas.

∎

Unmatched buffets, groaning sideboards, sofas, bentwood chairs, and a lone column un-

self-consciously mix in the light-filled sunroom, opposite. The patchwork lampshade has been in the family for some time. The collection of samovars grouped on a side table includes family heirlooms, a few country pieces, and a large one from an old tavern.

∎

BEREZHNAYA

SOME PEOPLE HAVE A GIFT FOR TAKING beauty where they find it. Child-psychologist Elinora Berezhnaya travels in her free time to different regions in search of folk art for her collection of wooden ware and toys. She started buying at exhibitions and later began seeking out artisans' work in the provinces. On each trip she buys as much as she can carry away at the time: "I never travel with empty suitcases to fill. That would bring bad luck. I carry boxes and wrappings with me and only a few personal things. I take just the dress I'm wearing. I wash it in the river, wait for it to dry, and put it on again!"

The look of the cooperative apartment into which Ms. Berezhnaya moved nearly twenty years ago is now cheerily dictated by her myriad small treasures. She claims to have loved every shade of red, from raspberry to tomato, before she began to collect, and red, the most typical color for painted wooden ware, predominates.

As her collection has grown, it has become more specialized. So have her means of display. A big catchall cabinet in the largest room is filled to its limit with some of the most common types of matryoshka dolls and wooden eggs. In another room she uses tapestries, quilts, and throw pillows in vibrant patterns and colors to create vignettes that draw the larger, more functional folk pieces into the overall decoration. Short stretches of wall in the hallway and kitchen prove just enough for all-of-a-kind groupings from a single region.

266

The objects, right, are lightly hand painted, playing up their uncolored clay bodies. The unusual, hook-nosed fantasy creatures were found in a Tadzhik village and are largely the work of one woman. Ms. Berezhnaya's own work, several pieces of needlework and a painting on wood, hangs alongside.
■

In a corner of one room, opposite, a trunk, chair, wooden plaques, and breadboards are from Gorodets. The hats hanging on the same wall are Uzbek and Tatar. On the adjacent wall, a brightly patterned carpet in similar tones complements the Khokhloma wooden ware in characteristic gold, red, and black from the town of Semyonov.

Overleaf: *A bookcase in the main room is devoted to folk objects from various areas: Polkhov-Midon (top shelf and bottom shelf, left, and small samovars and cups), Arkhangelsk (second shelf down, center), Uzbekistan (same shelf, left), Tadzhikistan (third shelf down, center), and Krutets (bottom shelf, right).*
■

A wine bottle painted by Ms. Berezhnaya and a basket she decorated with rowan berries stand on an oil cloth–topped windowsill, above left. In the kitchen, above right, many functional folk pieces are put to use. They include Uzbek and Tadzhik trays, pottery from Zhostovo, a blue-and-white tea service from Gzhel, and terra-cotta casseroles from Karelia.

■

Children's toys from the Gorky region top another bookcase, opposite. Folk art on the two shelves below is from Kaluga. The above painting of a house which Ms. Berezhnaya knows was presented to her as a gift by an artist in the Vologda region.

REZVIN

CONTENT TO COLLECT THE COMMON-place for his own home, Vladimir Rezvin spends his professional hours heading teams of restorers, unearthing finds of a more academically significant nature. His work has likely led him to some of the "throwaway" pieces that line his shelves at home. By registering his collection of everyday metalware and popular plaster-of-paris banks with the state, he was awarded precious storage space: two dank vaulted rooms in the basement of the building where he has an apartment.

Mr. Rezvin's taste runs from the general to the particular. On one shelf, slightly damaged samovars of different vintages crowd together, while throughout, pictures of Lenin and Stalin sidle up to pussycats, fruit bowls, and little girls bearing bright bouquets of flowers. Hundreds of turnkeys from old samovar spouts fill the space on a wall, while figurative paintings by unknown artists, printed pictures hand-colored by the deaf, and tea-glass holders have also found a home in this eclectic, idiosyncratic collection.

*M*r. Rezvin has constructed simple shelves to contain the abundance of metalware, ranging from samovars with missing parts to tea-glass holders and oil lamp bases, *right. His collection of banks is arranged around a door,* opposite. *Such pieces are hard to come by intact as so many*

were broken to empty them. The largest cat, to the right of the door, was made before 1917.

■

Overleaf: *Samovar turnkeys are given a wall of their own. Paintings are stacked wherever space allows in the basement display rooms.*

■

R E Z V I N

DOBROKHOTOVA

MANY OBSERVERS HAVE COMMENTED that women are the backbone of contemporary Soviet society. Here is a house of handmade pieces, reflecting the skills of three generations of women. It is occupied now by two sisters and one of their daughters: Tatiana, Natalya, and Valentina Dobrokhotova. All the members of their family have translated their artistry into bedspreads, wall coverings, throws, curtains, embroideries, lamps, furniture finishes, toys, and even educational devices, weaving them all together into the fabric of a warm, multihued living space.

The apartment house was developed twenty-five years ago outside central Moscow. Residents of the area count themselves lucky to live in one of the few complexes that combines small scale, postwar housing and expanses of greenery. In the quarter century since the first of them moved in, the trees and berry bushes then planted have flourished to become a welcome place for children to play and weary adults to rest at the end of a day.

The two sisters work as book illustrators; although one was trained as a chemist, she left that profession after one year. Walls crowded with pictures give evidence of every family member's confidence in her own expressiveness. Each helps to squirrel away fabrics, papers, wood, paints, and skeins of thread so fingers need not be idle when store supplies are scarce. Their mother contributed the patchwork bedspreads and the work of friends have their place here too.

276

A fantasy globe was made using collage by Natalya and Valentina, right. In one bedroom, opposite, a crocheted coverlet is layered with patchwork and embroidery. Behind it, a fabric hanging, depicting

a tree, turns the back of a bookcase into a headboard. Stacked on top of the bookcase are stage sets for tabletop theater with dolls. The child's chair has been used by all family members.

■

*H*omemade rag dolls and bits of hand-work contributed by each generation give this the air of a storybook house for children of all ages. Atop a quilt sewn by their mother, Natalya's and Tatiana's pillows are piled: the sausage shape uses fabric from an old shirt; the man is a char-acter from a fable.

■

In a corner of the main room, opposite, warm col-or and simple forms make a delightfully surrealistic setting for a workspace. The trompe l'oeil wall art was painted by Dmitri, Tatiana's son. Near a lampshade made by Tati-ana lies a partly complet-ed papier-mâché boat by Natalya. Their mother made the curtains.

FISHERMEN'S COTTAGES

OUTSIDE YALTA, CLIMBING THE EM-bankments of the Black Sea, are clusters of fishermen's cottages. Terraced into the hillside, the strips of land held back with weathered stone retaining walls are just wide enough to suit the small dwellings erected alone or in pairs. The mild southern climate casts an easy glow over the hard lives of the fishermen, who depend on the environment for their welfare.

The huts, fabricated simply of wood or of stucco over cement block, function as little more than basic shelter from inclement weather and sleeping places for the fishermen and their families. What the interiors of the dwellings do not provide can be compensated for by the plots of land at their doorsteps. Tables and chairs stabilized in the sandy dirt routinely accommodate outdoor meals. Even an outside kitchen may be shared by the inhabitants of two cabins. Paths between houses are made of boardwalk laid across dusty yards and plants create screens between huts for some-time seclusion. A lace curtain, strung across a small window, softens a façade, and paint in gay shades adds to the feeling of life.

A woman and her dog peer out of a vine-covered cottage, left. Inside another such dwelling, curtains give the only privacy between rooms, opposite. Beds are layered, in typical Russian fashion, with the plain linens available. A wall hanging alongside the bed helps to make it a sitting place too.

A *collage of humble materials and paint colors composes the house and porch railing, above. A hefty grapevine adds natural trim to the edge of the roof.*

■

Sea blues and greens are a natural here. A built-in bench and storage box extend the living space out onto a small mortar patio, opposite top. Tiles and shells are used as applied ornament to dress up homemade fittings. Oilcloth covers a cement-block work surface in an outdoor kitchen, opposite bottom. Jars and bottles are used for making juices and canning summer produce.

INDEX